JESUS

Centerpiece
of Scripture

TABLE OF CONTENTS

FOREWORD

*T*his book has been compiled from our library of Dr. McGee's messages preserved for us on audio cassettes. They have been selected with the intent of offering glimpses of who Jesus is so that we may stand in awe as we see Him "despised and rejected by men," yet always gracious and full of compassion, "slow to anger and of great mercy."

As the final chapter is edited and put in place, we find, as Dr. McGee has expressed it, that we are standing on the shore of an infinite sea! We feel like a little child playing with a bucket and a shovel, knowing nothing of those vast shores and that vast, heaving sea.

May the Holy Spirit push back the clouds and open our minds and hearts to continually grow in the knowledge and appreciation of this wonderful Person—Jesus, the centerpiece of Scripture.

—Trude Cutler, Editor

Chapter 1

WHO IS JESUS?

God, who at various times and in various ways spoke in time past to the fathers by the prophets, has in these last days spoken to us by His Son, whom He has appointed heir of all things, through whom also He made the worlds; who being the brightness of His glory and the express image of His person, and upholding all things by the word of His power, when He had by Himself purged our sins, sat down at the right hand of the Majesty on high, having become so much better than the angels, as He has by inheritance obtained a more excellent name than they. (Hebrews 1:1–4)

Y ou will notice that the first verse of the Book of Hebrews opens with the word *God*. Oh, this epistle opens on a grand scale! "God!" There is nothing before it to try to prove He exists. So our first assumption is that God exists. If you deny the existence of God, the problem is with you, not with God. So many little men who carry Ph.D. degrees deny that God exists. My thought is, *Who are they?* Put one of those puny little minds down by the side of God, and it becomes obvious why God did not waste His time proving who He is. I would like to refer them to God's question to Job: "Where were you when I laid the foundations of the earth?" If any person is going to come to God, that person must first believe that God is.

The second assumption is that God has spoken. Realizing that God is an intelligent person and that He has given mankind a certain degree of intelligence, if we didn't already have a revelation from Him, I would suggest that we wait for it. It is only logical that the Creator would get a message through to us. Well, my friend, He *has* communicated with us. And the revelation that we have is the inspired Word of God, the Bible. The first verse of the Book of Hebrews assumes that the Scriptures we have are divinely inspired. And He used different processes in communicating them to us. One time God would give a promise; another time He'd give a law; another time He'd give a dream; another time it was ritual. Another time it was history, another time poetry, and another time prophecy. Different ways, you see. So when you look back in the Old Testament, you recognize that God spoke, but He didn't give the Old Testament all at once. He did it in different ways over a period of nearly fifteen hundred years.

Then He stopped all of that, and after about four hundred years of silence we are told that "He has in these last days spoken to us by His Son." This is the reason I'm not interested in the *Koran* or *Science and Health* or *The Book of Mormon*. God now has spoken to us in His Son, and He hasn't any more to say. He's said it all in Christ. He has spoken fully and completely in Christ, and there is nothing more to follow. So if you have a vision, do not attribute that to a revelation from God. He's not speaking in dreams and visions anymore. Just think back to what you had for dinner. That may explain why you had a vision. God is speaking in His Word, and He's speaking through Christ today. Jesus is God's final Word. In these last days He has spoken to us by His Son. And literally it's not by *His* Son nor by *the* Son, and it's not even by *a* son. In the original Greek it is simply *in Son*. That's the only way God is speaking today. And this means that the writer is not putting the emphasis on the *person* of Christ, but on the *character* of Christ.

Now follow seven wonderful statements concerning the Lord Jesus Christ. First, *Whom He has appointed heir of all things.* In this we have the program for the future. For example, do you want to know who is ultimately going to control China? Or do you wonder who's going to get Europe or America? Well, Jesus Christ is. He's been appointed heir of all things. All will be coming to Him. The predestined end of this little world on which we live is that it is to come in under the reign of Jesus Christ. This makes me feel like shouting Hallelujah! The Lord God omnipotent will reign forever and ever! He is the heir.

Then will you notice the second thing: *Through whom also He made the worlds [made the ages].* The

Greek word for "worlds" is *aion*, and that means "ages." This is even more than physical; it is the time periods.

The Lord Jesus Christ is the creator of this universe, and there is purpose to it. Abroad today is the idiotic notion that the universe is running at breakneck speed through time and space like a car that has lost the driver. The interesting thing is that when a car loses the driver there is a wreck, but this universe, even according to the scientists, has been running for millions of years; and it has been doing pretty well, by the way. The sun comes up at a certain time every morning; it is very precise. The moon stays in a predictable orbit. As one of the men who worked on the moon modules said, "All they have to do is aim, and the moon will be there when the module gets there." You can always depend on the moon. It is not running wild. This is not a mad universe in which you and I live. It has purpose, and the Lord Jesus is the One who gives it purpose.

Why has everything been created as it is? My illustration is this: As you look into the night sky, do you see that little star on the end of the Big Dipper? I've often wondered why it is there. And I know now. It's there because He wanted it there. These things in His universe are there because He wants them that way. It's His universe. It's His right. If He wants a star there, He puts it there. He never asked any of us, and He's not apt to. Everything is resolved in the person of Christ.

Now notice the third wonderful thing about our Lord: *Who being the brightness of His glory.*

"Brightness" means the outshining of His glory, the effulgence. The material sun out in space gives us a good example of this. We could never know the glory of the sun by looking at it because we can't look at it directly—it would blind us if we tried. But from the rays of the sun we get light and we get heat. That is the way we know about the sun. Now in somewhat the same way we would know very little about God apart from the revelation that God has given in His Son. The Lord Jesus Christ is the brightness we see. No one has seen God, but we know about Him now through Jesus Christ. Just as the rays of the sun with their warmth and light tell about the physical sun, so also the Lord Jesus reveals God to us today.

The express image of His person. That phrase "express image" is the Greek *charakter*, the impressed character, like a steel engraving. We get our English word *character* from this. We say that the Lord Jesus Christ is the revelation of God because He *is* God. He is not just the printed material; He is the steel engraving of God because He is the *exact copy*, the image of God.

The Lord Jesus Christ is not only a man through whom God moved. He's not just a religious genius. He is God. You may recall that He said to His disciples, "He who has seen Me has seen the Father." For instance, when we see Jesus weeping at the tomb of Lazarus, we know how God feels when our loved one dies. Jesus is God manifest in the flesh. When He came to this earth, He was God, every bit God. Jesus is the express image of His person. Oh, how wonderful He is!

And upholding all things by the word of His power. Jesus Christ not only made everything, He not only entered the human family in a human body, but even as that little Baby yonder in the stable back of the inn, He was holding everything together. And if you don't think that takes power, consider the power in one atom when they split or untie it! That little fellow becomes dangerous! Well, who has them all tied together? Jesus Christ has. If He let go today—well, since you and I are held on this earth by His glue, His stickum, which we call gravitation—we would go flying out into space. This universe would come unglued without His constant supervision and power. He is not like an Atlas holding up the earth passively. He is actively engaged in maintaining all of creation. As far as I can see, that is greater than creating it in the beginning. He keeps the thing running, keeps it functioning. He's holding everything together by the word of His power. This is one of the tremendous things He is doing today.

At this point in Hebrews we reach the time of His incarnation, when He intruded Himself into human history at Bethlehem, and finally at Calvary. Which brings us to the sixth and greatest statement: *When He had by Himself purged our sins, sat down at the right hand of the Majesty on high.* No event of time or eternity can in any way compare with the tremendous significance of the death of Christ when He purged our sins. During those dark hours on the cross His righteousness and His love for the human family were supremely revealed.

"When He had by Himself purged our sins." Think of it, friends, the Lord Jesus Christ provided the cleansing for our sins! This, by the way, is the only purgatory mentioned in the Bible. He went through it for you and me; there is no purgatory for anyone who trusts Christ because He purged our sins. He has paid the penalty for them. How wonderful He is! The purging was accomplished by what He did on Calvary for you and for me, and today we are accepted in the Beloved. The one who comes to Christ receives a full redemption and complete forgiveness of sins. Oh, what a Savior!

"Sat down" does not indicate that He is resting because He is tired—or that He is doing nothing. It means that when He finished our redemption, He rested because it was complete; there was nothing more He needed to do.

As for me, there is always something incomplete—you should see my desk right now! My work is never complete, but Christ sat down because His work of redemption was complete. Friend, you cannot lift your little finger to add to the redemption He wrought for you on the Cross. He has completed our redemption, and we are complete in Christ. In Colossians 2:9–10 we are told, "For in Him dwells all the fullness of the Godhead bodily; and you are complete in Him, who is the head of all principality and power." We are made complete in Him, made full in Him, and we are accepted in the Beloved. How wonderful!

The present ministry of Christ is another aspect of this. He died down here to save us; He lives up there to keep us saved. He has a ministry of intercession, a ministry of shepherding, a ministry of disciplining His own. Although He is at God's right hand now, He is still vitally interested in those who are His own, and He is available to us.

My friend, what do you need? Do you need mercy? Do you need help? Do you need wisdom? Whatever you need, why don't you go to Him for it? If you ask Him to intervene in your behalf, He will work it out according to His will (but maybe not your will). Prayer is not to persuade God to do something that He didn't intend to do; prayer is to get you and me in line with the program of God. And Christ is at the right hand of the Father, ever living to make intercession for us. We can obtain mercy and find grace to help in time of need. This is the present ministry of Christ, and it makes these verses in Hebrews pretty real to you and to me.

This brings us to the seventh wonderful statement. Christ is not only better than the prophets of the Old Testament because He gives us a complete, full revelation of God, but He is also better than angels: *Having become so much better than the angels, as He has by inheritance obtained a more excellent name than they.* Christ is superior to the angels. Angels were prominent in their ministry to Israel in the Old Testament. And in the Book of Revelation we find that after the church is removed, there is an angel ministry of judgment that is going to take place.

In view of the growing prominence of angels in

our decadent culture, we need to keep in mind the warning of Galatians 1:8:

But even if we, or an angel from heaven, preach any other gospel to you than what we have preached to you, let him be accursed.

This verse is as strong as anything could possibly be. Paul says that if an angel dared to declare any other message than the gospel, he would be dismissed with a strong invective.

If an angel should appear to you or to me right now and say, "You are right as far as you go, but you also have to *do* something to be saved," both you and I should say, "Get out of here; I'm not listening to you although you might even be an angel from heaven." My friend, in our day we hear many folk who are trying to give us another "gospel." They may look like angels to you—after all, Satan himself is transformed into an angel of light, and his ministers are transformed as the ministers of righteousness (see 2 Corinthians 11:14, 15).

In Galatians 1:9, Paul goes on to say:

As we have said before, so now I say again, if anyone preaches any other gospel to you than what you have received, let him be accursed.

"Let him be accursed" is literally "let him be damned." Friend, I could not make that statement any stronger.

But to the Son He says:

**"Your throne, O God, is forever and ever;
A scepter of righteousness is the scepter of
   Your kingdom.
You have loved righteousness and hated
   lawlessness;
Therefore God, Your God, has anointed You
With the oil of gladness more than Your
   companions."** (Hebrews 1:8, 9)

By the way, this is a quotation from Psalm 45:6, 7 which reveals that it is one of the great messianic psalms. This One who is coming, according to the writer to the Hebrews, is the Lord Jesus Christ. He is the One who will rule. Imagine this old earth being ruled by One who loves righteousness and hates lawlessness and iniquity!

Your throne, O God. This is God the Father calling God the Son *God!* Do you want to deny that Christ is God manifest in the flesh? If you do, then may I say that you are contradicting God Himself. God called the Lord Jesus *God.* What are you going to call Him? I don't know about you, but I also am going to call Him *God.* He is God manifest in the flesh. He is far superior to angels because He is going to rule over the universe. He is the Messiah. He is the King of kings and Lord of lords who is going to rule over the earth someday.

Another tremendous passage sets before us the deity and the exaltation of our Lord Jesus Christ:

Therefore God also has highly exalted Him

and given Him the name which is above every name, that at the name of Jesus every knee should bow, of those in heaven, and of those on earth, and of those under the earth, and that every tongue should confess that Jesus Christ is Lord, to the glory of God the Father. (Philippians 2:9–11)

Hallelujah!

CHAPTER 2

CHRISTMAS IS GOD SHINING IN
From Eden to Bethlehem and Beyond

The first time that Christ came to this earth was not two thousand years ago at Bethlehem, but some six thousand years ago in the Garden of Eden.

An abnormal emphasis has been placed on the birth of Christ at Bethlehem. This emphasis has given us a rather warped conception of the thing that God would have us see in its proper perspective. We will not attempt to remove the luster from Christmas, the glory from Bethlehem, or the halo from the stable story. On the contrary, the birth of Christ will receive a new meaning which will shed new light upon the place where the star shone so brightly.

A pertinent question as we begin this subject is this: What do we mean by Christmas? Our forefathers came to this land of religious liberty in order to have a place where they could worship God according to the dictates of their conscience. Yet as I write this, our children in school are forbidden to hear the Christmas story as it is recorded in the only document, the Word of God. And they are forbidden to sing "Silent Night" and "Joy to the World." They can sing "Jingle Bells," however.

It is a pertinent question to ask. What do you mean by Christmas? Christmas means one thing and one thing only. We cannot indulge in some vague and vapid generalities like "the brotherhood of man" or have it dissipated and diluted with some sort of meaningless statement that has to do with "peace in our time." May I say, specifically, Christmas means the coming of Christ into the world in the flesh. And in particular it means the virgin birth of Christ.

Now our purpose in this message is to show that the first coming of Christ into the world was not two thousand years ago in Bethlehem but six thousand years ago plus! That's six thousand years at the minimum, and I think it was a great many more thousands of years that Christ came to the Garden of Eden! Christmas today, even as believers celebrate it, makes the coming of Christ to Bethlehem seem to be only a single such event. It's often said—you've heard it, I'm sure—"I cannot believe in the virgin birth because it's contrary to nature." Well, my friend, to be sure, it is contrary to nature. That's the whole point of it! Any manifestation of God's command is contrary to nature. And to bring up the fact that the queen bee is virgin born, as are certain other insects you can find in the biological world, proves nothing at all. Every time the supernatural touches the natural, it is not according to nature. And when God broke in after four hundred years of silence, it was with the words in Luke 2:10, "Do not be afraid . . . I bring you good tidings of great joy." Do not be afraid although the supernatural is touching the natural.

Epiphany: God Shining In

Now the real difficulty is not that the virgin birth is contrary to nature. It's the fact that folk are totally unaware that Christ came to this earth before Bethlehem. And the virgin birth is not just an isolated incident but is one in a series of events when Christ came to this earth. In the Old Testament Christ was there in history, and He was there in prophecy, and today we want to develop that even further.

Now again may I say that the critic has come forward with another objection—he has many, of course. I hear this each Christmas: If the virgin birth is so important, why didn't the apostle Paul mention it? The critic has made much of this. I heard it in college, I heard it in seminary, and I've heard it in the ministry ever since. My beloved, the fact of the matter is Paul *did* mention it, although he used another word, and I wish today we all could use that other word. Those of us who are not in a liturgical church are more or less inclined to push away from some very good Bible words. Here is one that Paul used several times. Notice his use of it in 2 Timothy 1:8–10:

Therefore do not be ashamed of the testimony of our Lord, nor of me His prisoner, but share with me in the sufferings for the gospel according to the power of God, who has saved us and called us with a holy calling, not according to our works, but according to His own purpose and grace which was given to us in Christ Jesus before time began, but has now been revealed by the appearing of our Savior Jesus Christ, who has abolished death and brought life and immortality to light through the gospel.

Notice that Paul has written, "but has now been revealed." The word "revealed" in verse 10 is translated from the Greek *phaneroo*. Then Paul continues, "God has now been revealed by the appearing," and "appearing" is *epiphaneia*, from which we get our word *epiphany*. Now *epiphany* is a word with which we are acquainted today. In fact, it is this Greek phrase that has been brought over into the English by transliteration. So, according to Paul, God has been revealed by the appearing of our Savior Jesus Christ.

The word *epiphany* means a shining in, and that's exactly the word that Paul uses. He uses other words for the coming of Christ, but *epiphany* is the one on which he dwells.

The fact of the matter is that Paul wrote of the two comings of Christ—His coming at Bethlehem and His second advent—and called each an epiphany when he wrote to a young preacher by the name of Titus: "For the grace of God that brings salvation has appeared to all men."

"The grace of God that brings salvation *has appeared*"—there's our word *epiphany*. When Christ came the first time it was God shining in.

Now will you notice God's instructions for today:

Teaching us that, denying ungodliness and worldly lusts, we should live soberly, righteously, and godly in the present age. (Titus 2:12)

Now for the future:

Looking for the blessed hope and glorious appearing of our great God and Savior Jesus Christ. (Titus 2:13)

And the word "appearing" again is the word *epiphany*. Paul said that when Christ came to Bethlehem some two thousand years ago, He was shining in— God was shining into this world. He's coming again, Paul reminds us, and when He comes, it will again be God shining into this world.

You'll find that the two advents, both the first advent and the second advent of Christ, are spoken of as epiphanies. And not only Paul but all the writers of the New Testament do this.

The apostle John, in 1 John 3:5, does as Paul does—he puts the two appearings right together:

And you know that He was manifested [there's

our word *epiphany*] **to take away our sins, and in Him there is no sin.**

That's the coming of Christ to Bethlehem. John here is making it very clear that it was God shining in, for that's the meaning of *epiphany. Phaneroo* means "to shine," and *epi* means "upon" or "into." *Epiphany* means the shining in of God into a darkened world. That's the reason John, in his Gospel, introduces the Lord Jesus as the Light. And of John the Baptist he said, "He was not that Light, but was sent to bear witness of that Light," and he added that "the true Light [Jesus] . . . gives light to every man coming into the world" (John 1:8, 9).

That was the first mention. But in 1 John 3:2 he says:

Beloved, now we are children of God; and it has not yet been revealed what we shall be, but we know that when He is revealed [there's our word again, *epiphany*]**, we shall be like Him.**

When He comes again it will be an epiphany. John and Paul and all the writers of the New Testament say that Christ's coming to Bethlehem was the shining in of God into this world. And when He comes again, it will be the shining in of God into this world.

It's interesting to note that historically the Greek Catholic Church refers to the baptism of Jesus as being the Epiphany. And you'll find that the Roman Catholic Church uses that word in connection with the wise men and especially the appearance of the star they followed.

We find the word *epiphany* used in reference to Christ's second coming, His second advent. And we find that the word *epiphany* is used at his birth in Bethlehem. Now think of the significance of this, my beloved: The appearance of that special star shining into this world was no accident. It was to be the herald, the sign of Christ's appearance. And that was the sign that the wise men had seen. It was the event that was to mark our Lord's shining into the world. His coming at Bethlehem was an epiphany, and the appearance of a star in the heavens was the proper place for it to be, for He had come out of heaven.

Now, friend, follow this carefully. It should give us a new appreciation and understanding of the preexistence of Christ. At His second advent, that is, when He comes again, it will be an epiphany. It will be an appearing from heaven, where He is now, and it will be His shining into this world.

His first advent was an appearing from a pre-existing state, and He was shining into this world. Each time He comes from heaven, each time He shines into this world, Paul says He is manifested in the flesh.

May I say, that's the way we describe the virgin birth. He was manifested in the flesh from an existence in heaven, and He came down to take upon Himself our human flesh. Let me now ask the real question: It is not how could He be born of a virgin, but how could He be born any other way? Could God have come into this world in human flesh any other way? Those who have raised the objection to the virgin birth, come forward now and tell me how God can shine into human flesh, take upon Himself our humanity, and be without sin. Impossible!

So you see that Paul does teach the virgin birth of our Lord, but he uses a different approach than we are used to. Unfortunately, we have dwelt too much on His humble birth in a stable when we should be emphasizing His deity, His shining in. His epiphany was the light of God breaking into the world. And the star was the herald, telling us that a little baby was the container for God!

Christmas Is Christ's Coming

The Old Testament is filled with appearances of God, and Paul identifies most of those appearances with the titles of Angel of the Covenant and the Angel of His Presence. Let's go back to the wilderness with Moses and the children of Israel. Paul said in 1 Corinthians 10 that the Rock that followed them was Christ. He sent the Angel of His Presence with them, and the Angel of His Presence was the One who led Israel by the cloud and the pillar of fire. It was none other than the preincarnate Christ who led Israel through the wilderness. This statement of the apostle Paul is of utmost significance, and the implications are tremendous. If Christ was the One in the greatest of the appearances of God in the Old Testament, then He is the One in the other appearances of God. This leads us to conclude that all of these manifestations of Christ in the Old Testament culminate in the Incarnation!

In the life of Jacob, two notable experiences are recorded in Genesis 28–32. One was at Bethel when he fled from home and from his brother Esau, and the other was at Jabbok when he fled from his father-in-law Laban. In the latter experience, Jacob had a very close contact with the Angel of the Lord in the wrestling match in which Jacob had no desire to participate. Later, in recounting the experience to the sons of Joseph, Jacob called him "the Angel who has redeemed me from all evil." Again, we have an appearance of the preincarnate Christ.

We can push further back in Genesis than Jacob to identify an appearance of Christ. "The Angel of the LORD" appeared to Abraham in his long experience of dealing with God. It is stated:

But the Angel of the LORD called to him from heaven and said, "Abraham, Abraham!" So he said, "Here I am." (Genesis 22:11)

This was during the ordeal of Abraham offering his son Isaac upon the altar. It was our Lord Jesus Christ who appeared to these men.

Now the question is, will the New Testament take us as far back as the Garden of Eden? If you follow me now, I'll take you to Christmas Day in the Garden of Eden. Notice Paul's language:

But I want you to know that the head of every

man is Christ, the head of woman is man, and the head of Christ is God. (1 Corinthians 11:3)

My beloved, the analogy here is that just as the woman was created from man and in the image of man, yet different, even so man was created in the image of Christ at the beginning. You must remember that our Lord is called "the last Adam." And back in the Garden of Eden, man had to be made in the likeness of Christ so that Christ might come in the likeness of man.

Christmas Is a Family Affair

Christmas Day in the Garden of Eden. Let's go back there. It's no "Jingle Bells" now. It's none of this modern folderol.

May I call your attention to something that is of tremendous significance and very interesting in Genesis 2:4: "These are the generations of the heavens and of the earth" (KJV). The more I study the Word of God, and the more I study the Book of Genesis, the more I'm convinced that Moses' concern was not in giving us the story of Creation—it's too brief to be the emphasis. He was not even concerned about giving details of the Flood—just a few facts; that's all. The important information he wanted to give us was the families. And what we have in the Book of Genesis, simply stated, is just the families.

As we look at these families, they become all-important. Look at this verse: "These are the generations of the heavens and of the earth." What does he mean by "the generations of the heavens and of the earth"? Notice that he begins immediately to talk about the creation of man in Genesis 2:7:

And the LORD God formed man of the dust of the ground, and breathed into his nostrils the breath of life; and man became a living being.

Man on the physical side is of the family of the earth. I repudiate the theory of evolution with all my being because when this man Adam began to look around for someone kin to him, somebody like him, he found none—not one.

And the LORD God said, "It is not good that man should be alone; I will make him a helper comparable to him." Out of the ground the LORD God formed every beast of the field and every bird of the air, and brought them to Adam to see what he would call them. And whatever Adam called each living creature, that was its name. So Adam gave names to all cattle, to the birds of the air, and to every beast of the field. But for Adam there was not found a helper comparable to him. (Genesis 2:18-20)

We are specifically told that among all the creatures that had been created there was not one found that could have fellowship with man, not one. But, my beloved, whether you like it or not, you have been taken out of the dust of the ground, and "dust you are, and to dust you shall return" (Genesis 3:19). On the physical side, that's all you are. The psalmist said, "He remembers that we are dust" (Psalm 103:14), but sometimes we forget it. And when dust gets stuck on itself, it's mud. You have in you today the same elements that are right out there in the dirt, and someday you'll go right back to it physically. "These are the generations of the heavens and of the earth."

But, you see, man is different. Man is not like the animals of the earth. Our Creator made man of the dust of the ground as He did the animals, but He didn't stop there. He breathed into his breathing places the breath of life, and man became a living soul. He is of the families of the heavens and of the earth.

Man has something of heaven in him, for God created him after His own image: "In the image of God He created him; male and female He created them" (Genesis 1:27).

I do not know in just what way this was true, but man in the image of God made it possible later on for Christ to come down and take upon Himself our human flesh. What a glorious, wonderful picture this is!

Several years ago scientists, after examining meteorites, came to the conclusion that life came from off this planet. Well, that's what God says in Genesis 2:7. God breathed into his nostrils or breathing places the breath of life, and man became a living soul.

Now follow this very carefully:

— 23 —

And the LORD God said, "It is not good that man should be alone; I will make him a helper comparable to him." (Genesis 2:18)

We live in a society that glorifies the independent wife who pursues her own career, but when any woman thinks she's something other than a helpmeet for her husband, she has missed her high calling. And too often the breakup of the family is the tragic result. Now that's old-fashioned, isn't it? But it's Bible.

Oh, my friend, how much better is God's plan! Now will you notice:

And the LORD God caused a deep sleep to fall on Adam, and he slept; and He took one of his ribs. (Genesis 2:21)

That's an unfortunate translation. Actually, the Hebrew words mean He took *one side* of man, implying that He took one half of man to make a woman. Let me give you a more literal translation:

And the LORD God caused a deep sleep to fall upon Adam, and he slept; and He took one half of Adam, and closed up the flesh instead thereof; and with this half, which the LORD God had taken from man, made He a woman, and brought her to the man. (vv. 21, 22)

She's like him, but she's different. And I want to say this: She was the most beautiful creature this world has ever seen. You've never seen any beauty in the daughters of Eve today but what Eve herself didn't combine with everything else. Adam fell for her. It was love at first sight. This is a marriage that I know was made in heaven. Some of them are not—they make them in another place. But this one was made in heaven.

> **And Adam said:**
> **"This is now bone of my bones**
> **And flesh of my flesh;**
> **She shall be called Woman,**
> **Because she was taken out of Man."**
> **Therefore a man shall leave his father and mother and be joined to his wife, and they shall become one flesh.** (Genesis 2:23, 24)

Marriage is not a union; it's unity. They become one. And the unity is seen in the child. God now has brought to Adam his other half. She is like him, and yet she's different. Paul said that as the man is the head of the woman, so Christ is head of the man. This is because man was first made in the image of God in order that the Son might be able to come down at Bethlehem and become a man.

May I say that when that first man was created, and then that first woman (I do not know this, I'm merely guessing now), I think the angels shouted for joy. It's not a baby now, born in a stable, but it's a man in the Garden of Eden. A man, may I say, in two halves. And he was in the image of God.

I wish I could say they lived happily ever after. That's not the way the story ends. It's a sad story. Genesis 3 is probably the most important chapter in the Bible because it tells the story of the entrance of sin and of death into the human family. Genesis 3 is the only way you can explain this world we live in today.

As we contemplate our Christmas this year, my friend, I do not think any person, regardless of how much rosewater he likes to use, can miss the fact that we are living in a crazy, mixed-up world. Constant threat of world war, men at each other's throats, problems that men cannot solve. Suffering everywhere; starvation; restlessness in the hearts of mankind; hospitals filled; mental institutions filled; homes broken; lives smashed. How do you explain it, brother?

Well, Genesis 3 explains it. We're right now in a struggle for our very existence. Sumner Wells, during World War II, said, "We have lived, and we are living, in a rotten world." He said that—I didn't say it. If that was true back during World War II, what is it today? May I say this, my beloved, if we are not now approaching the end of this age when the Lord intends to remove His own from this earth and begin His program of judgment, which will bring Him to the throne—if God does not intend to do that, I have an awful suggestion to make to you. He may let this world lapse again into the Dark Ages. The entire world can move back behind another curtain, and darkness again can cover this earth. It was back in the Middle Ages that a monolithic religious system of totalitarian dictatorship and darkness spread throughout the world. And if God is not getting ready to move again, we will go back into it, my beloved. It's not a pretty thought, is it?

Why is this true? Because of Genesis 3. This man and this woman doubted God. They didn't believe He'd do the best for them. Then they disobeyed God; they rebelled and ran away from Him. That's the picture, and it's been the picture ever since. That's the picture in your town and my town today. We are not running to God; we are running away from God!

The first Christmas message breaks in now. That first Christmas message was not "Merry Christmas!" It was a question, although it was not the one asked by the wise men, "Where is He who has been born King of the Jews?" That was man seeking God. But in the Garden of Eden it is God seeking man, and He cries out, "Adam, where are you?" That is the first Christmas message.

Here is the record in Genesis 3:8: "And they heard the sound of the LORD God walking in the garden in the cool of the day." The Lord Jesus Christ apparently was in the habit of coming at the conclusion of each day to talk with this man and this woman. They could have fellowship with Him, and He could have fellowship with them because they were in His image. The head of the man is Christ. The head of the woman is the man. And so one day He came as usual, but this time it wasn't as usual. This time when they heard the voice of the Lord God walking in the garden in the cool of the day, Adam and his wife hid themselves from the presence of the Lord God among the trees of the garden. And the Lord God called unto Adam and said unto him,

"Where are you?" He is not asking what tree he is hiding behind. God knew where he was. Rather, He was asking where he was now in relation to God. Where are you in relation to the world that you're in? Where are you?

Christmas Brings Gifts

God was looking for man. May I say, it was a glorious, wonderful day when, though man was in rebellion against God, had turned his back and run away from Him, God was still searching him out!

No room in the inn—little wonder. Did you expect there would be room for Him in Bethlehem's inn? Did you? No. From the very beginning man has been running from Him. And when He comes to Bethlehem, man shuts the door and says, "No vacancy, go somewhere else!" Well, our Lord is coming in. Even if He has to come in through a stable, He will come, for He's looking for man!

Do you want to know what the first Christmas gift was? We find it in Genesis 3:21: "Also for Adam and his wife the LORD God made tunics of skin, and clothed them."

Eve got a new fur coat for Christmas, and so did Adam. How did they get the coats? They got the coats because an animal was slain. That's the only way you can get the skin of an animal, isn't it? An animal had to be slain. Here's where the sacrificial system begins. This is the first Christmas gift.

Now we're told that this couple has to leave the

Garden, they cannot stay there and live forever. Thank God for that!

Let me ask you a question: Would you want to live as you are living now forever? I certainly wouldn't. God says to this man and this woman, "You'll have to get out; you'll not live forever. Death is come now."

So He drove out the man; and He placed cherubim at the east of the garden of Eden, and a flaming sword which turned every way, to guard the way to the tree of life. (Genesis 3:24)

Now a great many folk think this means that these cherubim were put there to keep man away. But, no, they were put there to keep the way open to God. And when Adam and Eve left the Garden of Eden, they turned and looked back, and when they turned, the sun was going down in the west, and between the two cherubim there was that glory, a shining light. The way to God was open because a sacrifice had been made, and they are now clothed with that which speaks of the righteousness of Christ.

We began with Paul, and we come back and close with him. In 2 Corinthians 8:9 Paul said:

For you know the grace of our Lord Jesus Christ, that though He was rich, yet for your sakes He became poor, that you through His poverty might become rich.

What a sublime act of impoverishment! He came

down to find man in the Garden of Eden. Epiphany. Any time He breaks through, epiphany! And about two thousand years ago, He broke through again in a stable—an epiphany. But you say, "I think I'm good enough!" Well, if you do, He didn't come for you. He came to seek and to save that which was lost.

For the grace of God that brings salvation has appeared to all men, teaching us that, denying ungodliness and worldly lusts, we should live soberly, righteously, and godly in the present age, looking for the blessed hope and glorious appearing of our great God and Savior Jesus Christ, who gave Himself for us, that He might redeem us from every lawless deed and purify for Himself His own special people, zealous for good works. (Titus 2:11–14)

CHAPTER 3

"GOD SO LOVED
THE WORLD . . ."
(JOHN 3:16)

God loves us!

There is a sinking feeling of total inadequacy as I come to this verse of Scripture. I am not able to communicate to you the vastness of the love of God, the intensity of that love, the overwhelming goodness of our God. Yet as you and I move into this new age in which a crisis looms as a cyclonic cloud in every direction, we need to know that God loves us. I pray that the Spirit of God will make this real to you; I am dependent upon Him.

In the original language, the Greek text, it reads like this:

For so loved God the world that He gave the Son, the only begotten one, in order that anyone believing into Him might not perish but have life everlasting.

The words are simple. In fact, as you read through the entire Gospel of John you will find that most of the words are monosyllabic. The words are so simple that a child can read them but so profound that I question if any one of us knows what they mean.

The emphasis is upon love. Notice in the Greek rendering that it reads, "loved God the world." In Greek sentence structure the important part of the sentence is placed first. In this verse actually *God* is not the important word, and *world* is not the important word; the important word is *loved*. The emphasis is upon the love of God.

The Imperative of Love

These words are a part of an interview that Nicodemus had with our Lord one night. They sum up all that previously had been covered in the conversation. Before we come to the words of our text, let us look at the two verses that immediately precede it, as they are very important to the understanding of it.

And as Moses lifted up the serpent in the wilderness, even so must the Son of Man be lifted up, that whoever believes in Him should not perish but have eternal life. (John 3:14, 15)

Notice that the Lord Jesus is calling Nicodemus's attention to something with which he is very familiar—the account in the Old Testament of the lifting up of the serpent in the wilderness. He said, "Even so *must* the Son of Man be lifted up." The *must* corresponds to the *must* that our Lord gave to Nicodemus at the very beginning of their conversation. He said, "You must be born again," and since you *must* be born again, then the Son of Man *must* be lifted up. The necessity of being born again makes imperative the lifting up of the Christ on the Cross. It is a divine compulsion.

Our Lord threw open the doors of heaven that night for Nicodemus (and for us), and we behold the King of Glory—not enthroned and crowned, but on a cross. It is an arresting fact that Christ revealed His death on the cross to Nicodemus on His first trip to Jerusalem, at the very beginning of His ministry. He did not reveal this to His own disciples until three years later, six months before He went to the Cross.

And, by the way, this is the answer to those who say that the Lord Jesus was caught in Jerusalem between the upper millstone of Roman power and the nether millstone of religious cupidity and died as a helpless victim. This obviously is not true since three years before, here in Jerusalem, He had told Nicodemus of His approaching death on the cross. If He had wanted to escape it, He could have stepped over into the East, into the Orient—where there were teeming millions in that day—and could have disappeared so that Rome and the religious rulers could never have touched Him. But that was not His thought, for He says here that He would be lifted up because *God loved the world*.

"Love" Is an Interesting Word

Love, on which the emphasis is placed, is an interesting word. In the Greek language there are three words that are translated into the English by the one word *love*. This reveals how barren the English language is. Hollywood would give a million dollars if it had another word for *love*. But the Greeks had three words for it. One was *eros*, from which we get our word *erotic*, that is, sensual love. This is never used in the New Testament. Then there is the word *phileo,* which does appear in the New Testament, and its highest meaning is "friendship." It means, "I like you," and it means no more. Obviously this is not the word used here, because you cannot say that God so *liked* the world! The other word, the word used in John 3:16, is *agapao*, which is love in the highest degree. *Agapao* is an attribute of God; it is divine love, not human love. It is love lifted to a high, noble, supernatural plane. God loved!

The "world" means the ordered world in which we live. It means the world of mankind, and it means all men—it is not limited to the elect only; it is not limited to the good, it is not limited to any particular race—it encompasses the totality of the human race, from Adam right down to the present generation. Those who maintain that God loved only certain ones, only the elect, are not giving us the language of the Bible. God says that He loves all of the human family. No one is excluded.

Another great statement in this verse is "He gave." His love was revealed in the fact that He gave. Again there is the thought of totality; it was a total gift. It does not say that God gave His Son to die, although this is included, but it means more than that. It means that Christ's coming into the world about two thousand years ago—beginning with His virgin birth and ending with His death, His resurrection and ascension into heaven, even His present ministry today and His coming again in the future—is God's gift.

A great deal has been made of the words "only begotten Son." In the original language it does not say that God gave *His* only begotten Son—He did not beget Him. Rather, it is *the Son the only begotten one*, which is His title.

John begins his Gospel by presenting Jesus Christ as the eternal Word. Of Him he writes:

> **In the beginning was the Word, and the Word was with God, and the Word was God. He was in the beginning with God. All things were made through Him, and without Him nothing was made that was made.** (John 1:1–3)

In the beginning *was* the Word, not *is* the Word. It was not in the beginning that the Word started out or was begotten. "Was" is a durative imperfect, meaning continued action. It means that the Word *was* in the beginning. You see, we are dealing with the God of eternity. At the time of Creation "all things were made through Him, and without Him nothing was made that was made." No matter how far back you want to go, billions of years *before* Creation, the Son comes out of eternity to meet you. He was already there when the beginning was. The eternal Son, the Creator of all things, took upon Himself human flesh.

"The only begotten" is unique; it means that the Lord Jesus is unique. It was the same in the Old Testament. For instance, in Psalm 22:20 "My darling" or "precious" is "My only one." He was the only one in His birth—only He is virgin born. He was the only one in the life that He lived—only He lived a perfect life. It is only of Christ that the Father has been able to say, "This is My beloved Son in whom I am well pleased." He never has said that about you, and He never has said that about me—He could not say it—but He did say it of Christ. He is the only one who could die for the sins of the world. He is the only one who is back from the dead in a glorified body. He is today the only hope of the world, the only begotten Son.

Putting the Yardstick on "So"

Let's come back to our little word *so*. God *so* loved. How much is that? Let me give a little different translation of it to widen out that word: "God loved to such an astounding and astonishing degree." Now we are faced with a problem. Is there some way to bring this word *so* out of heaven and reduce it to the terminology of earth? Can we bring this little word down here and give it an incarnation so we can look at it? How much did God love the world?

Paul tells the Ephesian Christians that he prays this for them:

[That you] may be able to comprehend with all the saints what is the width and length and depth and height—to know the love of Christ which passes knowledge; that you may be filled with all the fullness of God. (Ephesians 3:18, 19)

Can we measure the love of God? Can we put down the yardstick on that little word *so* and determine the breadth of it and the length of it and the depth of it and the height of it? At this point I really feel inadequate. How can mere man measure the love of God?

Wide as "Whosoever"

Let us first try to comprehend the breadth of the love of God. How wide is His love? God's arms encompass the entire world so that all are included. And when it says that He loves all, it means that He loves each one—He loves *you*. And I frankly feel that John 3:16 is the most personal verse in the Bible; it is personal to you, and it is personal to me. It is more personal than if it said, "God so loved Vernon McGee." I'll tell you why.

Several years ago I was conducting meetings in a church in Seattle. One morning at the hotel where

I was staying, I received a telephone call from a woman who began speaking as if she knew me very well, "Pastor McGee, how are you?"

"Fine."

"How is Annie?"

"Annie?" I repeated, "I don't know Annie."

"Oh, yes, your wife."

"No," I countered, "you are wrong. I do not have a wife named Annie."

Suspiciously she probed, "Aren't you Vernon McGee?"

"Yes."

"Aren't you a preacher?"

"Yes."

"Were you not," she asked distrustfully, "pastor of a certain Methodist church back in Iowa?"

I said, "No ma'am. I never have been off the train in traveling through Iowa."

Puzzled, she continued, "Well, I knew a Vernon McGee who was a Methodist preacher, and he was my pastor back in Iowa."

"I'm sorry. I didn't know there was another one loose."

Now you know the reason I am glad that John 3:16 does not read, "God so loved Vernon McGee," because it might mean that other fellow and not me at all. But when it says, "God so loved the world," that means me and it means you.

God loves the world. We have heard this so much it is commonplace. But let me ask you: How could He love this reeking world today with all of its sin, its rebellion, its meanness, its ugliness, and its sor-

didness? Oh, He might love some folk who are lovely
and cultured and educated. But can He love those
savages in Africa who ate the livers of their captives?
Yes, He loves them exactly as much as He loves you.
God loves the meanest, lowest man you can think of
as much as He loves you—just as much. If you somehow think that you are one of God's little pets and that
He has placed His love on you and your kind and upon
no one else, you are wrong. God loves the world. God
made a level place at the Cross, which is the only place
where you have real integration. None is righteous
there; all have sinned. God declares all to be sinners
that He might have grace upon all.

**And He Himself is the propitiation for our
sins, and not for ours only but also for the
whole world.** (1 John 2:2)

God has His arms outstretched to a gainsaying, lost,
rebellious world. They spat in His face when He was
here, and they are still spitting in His face today.
Yet He says, "I love them."

A young fellow in my Southland was asked, when
he was being examined for church membership,
"How did you get saved?" He answered, "I did my
part, and God did His part." They thought they had
found a flaw in his theology and probed, "What was
your part, and what was God's part?" He answered,
"My part was the sinnin' and His part was the
savin'. I done run from Him as fast as these sinful
legs and this sinful, rebellious heart could carry me,
and He done took out after me 'til He done run me

down." And, my friend, that is the only way any of us is saved. God has pursued us because He loves us.

Years ago in England when the Quaker movement was new—and oh, what a warm movement that was at the beginning—Miles Halhead, a young married preacher, went everywhere with the message of Christ. Finally his wife in vexation exclaimed, "Would God I had married a drunkard that I might find him in the alehouse, but now I cannot tell where to find him—he goes everywhere preaching the gospel!" He had the love of Christ in his heart because God loves everybody. There is no exception. Oh, the breadth of the love of God!

Length by Demonstration

What about the length of God's love? God so loved that He gave. The test of love is to what length it will go. Love is not love which will not die or make sacrifices often more bitter and cruel than death. I always suspected that boy who sent a note over to his girl:

> I love you. I would climb the highest mountain for you. I would swim the deepest river for you. I would go through snow and hail for you.
> P. S. If it does not rain Wednesday night, I'll be over to see you.

May I say to you, we *demonstrate* our love. And God has demonstrated His love by the extent to which He has gone—He gave His Son. Do you want to know how much God loves you? Do you want to know the length to which He has gone? Listen to this:

For when we were still without strength, in due time Christ died for the ungodly. For scarcely for a righteous man will one die; yet perhaps for a good man someone would even dare to die. But God demonstrates His own love toward us, in that while we were still sinners, Christ died for us. (Romans 5:6–8)

God commends or proves His own love toward us, in that, while we were yet sinners, Christ died for us. What a staggering demonstration of His love!

God is on the giving end. He is not asking one thing from man. I am afraid we preachers give the wrong impression that God is asking this world for something. He asks nothing from this world! He said, "If I were hungry, I would not tell you; for the world is Mine, and all its fullness" (Psalm 50:12). If He wanted gold, would He ask us for the puny amount we have at Fort Knox today? Why, the gold and the silver are His, and the cattle on a thousand hills. God says in effect, "I do not want anything from you, but I would like to *give* you something: eternal life in Christ Jesus." God so loved the world that He gave, and He gave His only begotten Son. He gave Him not only at Bethlehem, not only in a perfect life, not only to teach, not only to reveal God, but He gave Him to die upon the cross for the sins of the world. My friend, what else can you ask Him to do for you?

Can you think of anything more that God could do for you, a sinner, than to give His Son to die for you that He might save you?

> *Love ever gives,*
> *Forgives*
> *Outlives,*
> *And ever stands*
> *With open hands.*
> *And while it lives,*
> *It gives.*
> *For this is love's prerogative:*
> *To give and give and give.*

I was interested in an article that appeared in a metropolitan newspaper some time ago. There was a picture of a mother and son with the caption "Father Gives Life for Son":

> Sidney Lawrence underwent a cross transfusion for his son, Robert . . . in which blood of father and son mingled. The father's kidney worked for both, allowing the son's diseased kidney to recuperate. But the father was sensitive to proteins in his son's blood, causing his death.

That man did not have to stand up and say, "I love my son." He proved it when he gave his life for his boy. There is many a father who would do that. But, my friend, God has gone far beyond that. He has given His *Son* to die for *you*. Do you want to ask Him to do something else? He has gone the very length of love.

Deep as Hell

Now let us attempt to ascertain the depth of God's love: "That whoever believes in Him *should not perish*." I don't want to be unloving and unkind to you, but someone needs to speak plainly. We are hell-doomed and hell-deserving sinners, every one of us. A great many folk think that mankind is on trial, that God wants to see if we will do better or not. This is not so. Notice the verses that follow our text:

For God did not send His Son into the world to condemn the world, but that the world through Him might be saved. He who believes in Him is not condemned; but he who does not believe is condemned already, because he has not believed in the name of the only begotten Son of God. (John 3:17, 18)

"He who believes in Him is not condemned." Well, suppose he does not believe in Him? He is already condemned. Why? Because mankind today is not a prisoner at the bar awaiting trial to see whether he is guilty or not. Mankind today is a prisoner inside the prison of this world, in sin, and is asked if he will accept a pardon. Someone says, "You don't mean to tell me that nice, sweet Mrs. So-and-So is lost!" My friend, she is a sinner in rebellion against God; she has no capacity for God; she would wreck heaven if she were permitted there without a new nature. "Well," someone asks, "what about the heathen who have never heard of Christ?" They are lost; *we are all born lost!* You and I are members of a lost race, a doomed race, and what Christ did was to come into this prison and say to men, "Do you want a pardon? I'll pay your penalty. I'll stay here and go through this hell for you."

For God did not send His Son into the world to condemn the world, but that the world through Him might be saved. (John 3:17)

He has done this because He loves you. God asks, "Why will you die?" The Lord Jesus says, "You will not come to Me, that you might have life."

Oh, the lovely thing that is said of the Lord Jesus Christ in Luke's Gospel, "He entered and passed through Jericho." Why? Because in Jericho there lived the chief of the publicans, a base sinner, a crook, and our Lord was going there to save him. He entered and passed through; He did not stay there. He did not even spend the night. He was there only long enough to win Zacchaeus. You can widen that out. Our Lord entered and passed through this world—John's Gospel gives the tremendous movement—Jesus said, "I came forth from the Father and have come into the world. Again, I leave the world and go to the Father" (John 16:28). He entered and passed through this world. Why? Because you were here and He wanted to save you. Don't tell me that He did not die for you; He died for *you*. He did this that you might not perish.

Immeasurable Height

What about the height of the love of God? "They shall have *everlasting life!*" The height is infinite. May I be personal again? I am going to heaven someday. You may think, "Well, you must be very good." On the contrary, I am not very good. I am going to heaven someday because Christ died for me and I have trusted Him.

We have not scaled the heights; we have not plumbed the depths of the love of God; we have not widened this out as it should be. Paul was accurate when he said, "To know the love of Christ that *passes knowledge.*" I am not able to measure the vastness or the intensity or the overwhelming goodness of God. If I could, it would break your heart, and it would break mine if I fully knew. I can only say that God loves you.

These are days in which a great many people are called to go through dark nights and deep waters. When you face problems and face them alone, you need to know that God loves you. Whoever you are, wherever you are, God loves you, and His love is revealed in Christ on the Cross. And, my friend, you will find it only there. It is not on the mountaintops or on the surging sea; it is not in babbling brooks or majestic redwood trees—you will not find it anywhere in nature. The Bible makes this crystal clear. "God so loved the world that He gave redwood trees and babbling brooks"? No, sir! "God *so* loved the world that He gave His only begotten Son, that whoever believes in Him should not perish but have everlasting life."

CHAPTER 4

WHY JESUS WAS TEMPTED

As we come now to the temptation of our Lord, we need to realize that there is a frightful and fearful darkness about the temptation and an appalling enigma associated with it. There is that which you and I will not be able to penetrate. I find there are three experiences in the life of our Lord that leave me on the outside. The first is here in the temptation. The second is in the Garden of Gethsemane, and the third is at the Cross. These are three events that I am not permitted to enter in too close, for unseen and hidden forces of evil were at work there. At these times He was surrounded by the powers of darkness and destruction, and we see Him grappling with the basic problems of mankind.

We are told in 1 Corinthians 15:47 that "the first man was of the earth, made of dust; the second Man is the Lord from heaven." But out there in the wilderness we find the Lord from heaven down yonder where it's earthy, laying hold of humanity that He might solve humanity's problems. He is down on the level where we are, and here God the

Son won a victory for mankind—for you and for me—in the temptation.

Preliminaries

Now there are several preliminary considerations that we want to look at before we examine the temptation itself.

We find that the Gospel according to Luke presents the Lord Jesus as the Son of Man. And it is very interesting that just before he records the temptation of Jesus, he gives us a genealogy, and it's the genealogy of Mary, the mother of Jesus. This is the genealogy from which our Lord got His humanity. And it is traced back, not only to David and even beyond Abraham, but it goes all the way back to Adam, for in Luke 3:38 the genealogy concludes: "The son of Enosh, the son of Seth, the son of Adam, the son of God." So we see that the genealogy which is given here is the genealogy that goes back to Adam. Then immediately the temptation of our Lord is given, for He was a man, and as a man, He "was in all points tempted as we are, yet without sin" (Hebrews 4:15).

Led of the Spirit

Will you note verse 1 of Luke 4:

Then Jesus, being filled with the Holy Spirit, returned from the Jordan and was led by the Spirit into the wilderness.

Now I'm confident you have noticed that He was filled with the Holy Spirit. The Son of God needed to be filled with the Holy Spirit in order to meet this temptation. If *He* needed to be filled with the Holy Spirit in order to be able to meet the temptation, I might as well face up to the fact—and you might as well join with me—that you and I cannot face the temptations of this world today in our own strength. You and I are joined in a battle in which we are hopelessly outnumbered, and we will be miserably defeated if we go forth in our own strength and with our own ability.

Paul could say, even as a believer after his conversion:

I find then a law, that evil is present with me, the one who wills to do good. (Romans 7:21)

In other words, Paul was saying, "After I became a child of God through faith in Christ, with a new nature that wanted to serve God, even at the very moment when I wanted to do good, evil was present with me. When I want to do good, evil is right there." I wonder if that has been your experience.

Again Paul could say:

For what the law could not do in that it was weak through the flesh, God did by sending His own Son in the likeness of sinful flesh, on account of sin: He condemned sin in the flesh, that the righteous requirement of the law might be fulfilled in us who do not walk ac-

cording to the flesh but according to the Spirit. (Romans 8:3, 4)

Paul found out that in and of himself he could not live the Christian life at all. He could not meet and grapple with the issues of life, for in his flesh there was nothing good. And even though Paul approved of the Law, he was unable to keep it because of the weakness of the flesh. But he found out that by walking in the Spirit of God he was enabled to live for God. That's the reason he could write to the Galatians:

I say then: Walk in the Spirit, and you shall not fulfill the lust [the desire] **of the flesh.** (Galatians 5:16)

Walk by means of the Holy Spirit! You and I, as we walk out of our homes and even a house of worship into the world, we will not live for God unless we walk in the Spirit, my beloved. If it's going to depend upon your feeble ability and my feeble ability, we'll fail before the sun goes down today. We cannot make it—we are unable to do it. Our Lord was filled with the Holy Spirit before He entered the wilderness.

Then we're told something else, that He was led by the Spirit into the wilderness. It's interesting to note that Mark, in his very brief and blunt record, says that "immediately the Spirit drove Him into the wilderness" (Mark 1:12). The word in the Greek is *ekballo*, which means "to throw out." The Holy

Spirit threw Jesus out into the wilderness. It all implies simply this: He did not seek the temptation. His attitude at the time of the temptation was the same as it was yonder in the Garden of Gethsemane when He prayed, "Let this cup pass from Me."

Any person in the flesh today, in the battles of life, is foolish to say that he can meet temptation and come off the victor. Even our Lord prayed, "Let this cup pass from Me." But He also hastened to add, "Nevertheless, not as I will, but as You will" (Matthew 26:39). May I say to you, that's His attitude here when He's driven, thrown out, into the wilderness by the Spirit of God. That's the first thing for us to note.

Satanic Purpose

The second thing that is preliminary is found in Luke 4:2:

Being tempted for forty days by the devil. And in those days He ate nothing, and afterward, when they had ended, He was hungry.

First off, let me say that the temptation did not begin at the end of forty days. Luke makes it very clear that during all forty days our Lord was tempted in a special way. But may I also add that the temptation did not start at the beginning of the forty days. All of His life, from the moment He was born and Herod sought to destroy Him, Satan was making attacks on Him. And when He concluded this temptation in the wilderness, that did not conclude His temptation as far as Satan was concerned. Luke is very careful to say:

Now when the devil had ended every temptation, he departed from Him until an opportune time. (Luke 4:13)

I believe that all through His ministry you find Him being tempted, even saying to Simon Peter, "Get behind Me, Satan" (see Matthew 16:23), recognizing that Satan was responsible for Peter's being deceived. It was in the Garden of Gethsemane under the shadow of the Cross that the tempter came to offer the Lord once again the crown without the Cross.

And He was withdrawn from them [His disciples] **about a stone's throw, and He knelt down and prayed, saying, "Father, if it is Your will, take this cup away from Me; nevertheless not My will, but Yours, be done."** (Luke 22:41, 42)

The cup, I think, was the Cross, and I do not mean the suffering of death. The cup was that He was made sin for us. He is the Holy One of God. When my sin was put upon Him, it was repulsive and awful. It was terrible, and for a moment He rebelled against it. The Lord, however, had come to do His Father's will and so He could say "nevertheless not My will, but Yours, be done." He committed Himself to His Father's will, although bearing your sin and mine was so repulsive to Him.

Then an angel appeared to Him from heaven, strengthening Him. (Luke 22:43)

There was an angelic ministry at the time of our Lord's temptation in the desert. Now there is an angelic ministry in the garden when Satan comes to tempt Him again. Luke alone recalls this fact.

And being in agony, He prayed more earnestly. Then His sweat became like great drops of blood falling down to the ground. (Luke 22:44)

Only Dr. Luke tells us that the Lord sweat great drops of blood. The Lord showed a tremendous physical reaction to the agony and conflict that confronted Him. I cannot explain what happened and do not propose to try. I am not, however, impressed by the biological explanations offered today. I realize that there are some wonderful Christian doctors who have come up with some interesting explanations, but I still am not impressed. He shed His blood for me, and I bow in reverence and worship.

But none of the ransomed ever knew
How deep were the waters crossed,
Nor how dark was the night that the Lord passed
   through,
Ere He found His sheep that was lost.

—Elizabeth C. Clephane, from
"The Ninety and Nine"

But, my beloved, our Lord went to the Cross with joy to be the sacrifice for your sins and for my sins! Oh, my friend, don't turn your back on a Savior who loves you like this! It will be tragic indeed if you do.

Looking unto Jesus, the author and finisher of our faith, who for the joy that was set before Him endured the cross, despising the shame, and has sat down at the right hand of the throne of God. (Hebrews 12:2)

A Personal Devil?

Now there is another matter of introduction: Is the devil a person or not? Is it just mythology, folklore, to say there's a personal devil? Or does Satan represent merely an influence of evil? Is it something that is merely psychological?

Ministers are greatly divided on this issue. Some time ago a poll of ministers in the Chicago area and in the New York area revealed that 30 to 90 percent—according to the area polled—believed there is no such thing as a personal devil. I do not know what the percentage is now. But, my friend, to say there is no such thing as a personal devil is to disbelieve the Bible. You may not believe the Bible, but if you do, you must recognize that the Word of God makes it clear that Satan is a person.

Since Satan is a spirit, an angel of light, the question is, of course, did he come in a bodily form to tempt Jesus? I believe he did come in bodily form. I think Christ met him face to face. The subtlety of Satan is that there are times he comes as a roaring lion, and other times he comes like an angel of light. He changes his method continually.

Tested or Tempted?

There's one other item that we need to note. We're told here that our Lord was tempted, "Being tempted for forty days by the devil." What do we mean when we say that Christ was tempted? That word has a twofold meaning, and we have to be very careful how we use it. To tempt someone can mean inciting and enticing to evil, especially to immorality. To tempt someone can mean to seduce that person, and the minute you say that, you are saying that there's something in the individual that causes him to succumb and yield to that sort of thing. But we know that was not true of Christ. His temptation was not that kind of temptation. He said in John 14:30, "For the ruler of this world is coming, and he has nothing in Me." Believe me, brother, when the tempter comes to you and me he finds plenty! But when he came to our Lord, he found nothing in Him. That is, there was no hook or handle that he could take hold of. So our Lord was not tempted in that sense at all. Hebrews 7:26 tells us He was "holy, harmless, undefiled, separate from sinners."

But the word *tempt* is used in another way in the Word of God. It is used, for instance, back in the Old Testament when it says, "God did tempt Abraham." Did God tempt Abraham to do something evil? No sir! God never tempts anyone with evil. Never. God did not tempt Abraham in that sense. What God did was test Abraham, and that's something altogether different. God tested Abraham.

Also God tested the children of Israel. After they had come through the wilderness, Moses gave them a resumé of the journey, and he said this:

And you shall remember that the LORD your God led you all the way these forty years in the wilderness, to humble you and test you, to know what was in your heart, whether you would keep His commandments or not. (Deuteronomy 8:2)

The forty years in the wilderness was a temptation to Israel. What sort of temptation? It was a test to see whether they would keep God's Law or not. Of course, they failed. That generation was not even permitted to enter into the Promised Land.

Now our Lord was tested. That raises the question. Could Christ have fallen? There's a great deal of difference of opinion here today. Could Christ have yielded to Satan's suggestions when He was tempted? May I say to you, the answer is a categorical no. He could not fall! Well, somebody says, then was it a legitimate temptation? Yes, it was a test, a test to demonstrate that He could not fall, that He was the immaculate Son of God, that He was an impeccable Savior, that He was able to save to the uttermost those who come unto God through Him. It was a demonstration.

Now that's not contrary to our way of living, even today. New articles are tested. Automobiles are tested, and tires are tested. If you should go to a site where one of the tire companies has a testing ground for their tires, and if you should stop and say, "What are you trying to do, ruin them?" they would say, "Oh, no. We're just proving that they cannot be ruined."

Let me give this very homely illustration. When I was a boy I lived in a west Texas town that is no longer on the map. Nothing is there now but mesquite bushes. But there was a time when those who founded the town had high hopes it would become a booming town. It never did. The little town was named Burnham. It was on the Santa Fe Railroad, right by the west fork of the Brazos River. The Brazos River is unusual in that during summertime you can't find enough water to wade in it. In fact, in late summer a mosquito couldn't even get a drink in it. But in the wintertime you could float a battle-ship up the river.

One year we had a flood. It washed out the bridge for the Santa Fe tracks, so the company came in and built a new strong bridge. When they had finished it, they ran in two locomotive engines on top of that bridge and tied the whistles down. All of us who lived in the little town—all twenty-three of us—ran down there because we'd never heard two whistles at the same time. Several officials of the Santa Fe were present for the occasion, and the engineer who had built the bridge was there. So one of the citizens of our community stepped up to him and asked, "What are you doing?"

"We're testing the bridge."

Of course, this citizen of our community went on to ask, "Are you trying to break it down with those two engines?"

This engineer with great disdain looked at him, actually with contempt, "Of course not. Two engines could never break down that bridge!"

"Then why in the world are you putting them on there?"

"We're putting them on to demonstrate that two engines cannot break the bridge down."

Our Lord was tempted for that same reason. And, my friend, because of that fact, He was tested in a way that you and I have never been tested. The pressure on Him was greater than it's ever been on any of us. For you and me, when the pressure builds up from temptation, we give way, and the minute we give way the pressure is relieved. But our Lord never gave way, and the pressure continued to build up. You and I really don't know what extreme temptation is as He knew it.

He knew what even Adam didn't learn. Adam, created innocent, never knew what it was to resist to the very end. Adam gave way to sin. You and I give way to sin, and the pressure is removed. Jesus never gave way, and the pressure built up. Only He knows what it was to really be tempted.

A Look at the Temptation of Christ

Now will you look with me at His temptation.

Then Jesus, being filled with the Holy Spirit,

returned from the Jordan and was led by the Spirit into the wilderness, being tempted for forty days by the devil. And in those days He ate nothing, and afterward, when they had ended, He was hungry. (Luke 4:1, 2)

I must confess that I cannot explain it, but I will take you to the very edge and hope we can learn something more about our Lord.

The attack that was made upon Him was in three areas of His complex personality. And the attack that has been made upon you and me has always been made in these three areas, and it is being made there today. The attack is on the body, that which is physical; upon the mind, that which is psychological; and upon the spirit, the will of man. There is a remarkable correspondence between the temptation of Adam, the temptation of Christ, and your temptation and mine today. Also there is a contrast. Our father Adam in the Garden of Eden was tempted under favorable circumstances and in a perfect environment. Our Lord was tested out yonder in the wilderness under unfavorable—in fact, very harsh—circumstances.

Physical Temptation

Now will you notice these three testings. The first is physical. Remember that the powerful satanic forces of evil were surrounding Him and bearing down on His weakened body—without food for forty days!

And the devil said to Him, "If You are the Son of God, command this stone to become bread." (Luke 4:3)

Now there's nothing particularly evil in that as you look at it. Satan didn't ask Him to make alcohol; he didn't ask Him to make dope. He didn't ask Him to commit an obvious sin. All he did was ask our Lord to make those stones lying at His feet into bread. That was all. And there is nothing wrong with bread. The Scripture says bread is the staff of life, that it's a necessity. On one occasion Jesus fed five thousand people, and at another time He fed four thousand, and He did it miraculously. Why not do it here?

It's the same temptation that came to Eve in the Garden of Eden when she looked at the fruit hanging from the forbidden tree. She saw that it was good for food. There was nothing wrong with the tree or the fruit in and of itself. When Adam and Eve ate of the fruit of that tree, they did not suffer from ptomaine poisoning. The tree, I'm willing to concede, may have had the best fruit in the Garden of Eden— nothing wrong with it. The thing that was wrong was that God said not to eat of it.

What was wrong with our Lord making the stones into bread? Well, my beloved, the wrong thing was that it exemplified Satan's philosophy, which is still in existence today and by which most men live. It's simply this: A man must live, and in order to live he must eat. The most important thing in this life is to live and to eat. The clamor of the crowd and the medley of the mob is: *What shall we eat?* and *what shall we drink?* and *what shall we wear?* And in Southern California there are at least a thousand restaurants and five thousand supermarkets that answer your first question, *What shall we eat?* They are in business to answer that question.

There are thousands of liquor stores and cocktail lounges that want to answer the question, *What shall we drink?*

What shall we wear? Well, clothing stores abound, and they have the answer to that.

And you and I live in a society, a satanic society, where people will sell liquor and dope for money because *they've got to eat.* Folk will be dishonest. They'll steal; they'll gamble; they'll do anything for a dollar, *because they've got to eat.* This is Satan's low estimate of the human family. He has nothing in the world but utter contempt for us today! Why in the world would we serve him when he absolutely despises us? He said in Job 2:4, "All that a man has he will give for his life." The inference is that man is physical, only an animal, that's all. But Satan was wrong about Job.

Now listen to our Lord as He answers him.

But Jesus answered him, saying, "It is written, 'Man shall not live by bread alone, but by every word of God.'" (Luke 4:4)

Our Lord uses the sword of the Spirit, the Word of God. Then He makes this statement, that man is more than physical. After he's satisfied his hunger and he's slaked his thirst and he's dressed up like a peacock, down deep underneath there's still that which needs to be satisfied. He is more than physical. He's more than an animal.

Well, my friend, if man is only an animal we would be better off being a four-legged hog rather than a two-legged hog—we could eat more, sleep more, and grunt more. But we are more than the physical: "Man shall not live by bread alone, but by every word of God." Nothing in the world can satisfy the human heart except the Word of God.

Have you noted that the restless multitudes rush to and fro in this world, traveling everywhere? Every magazine that I see advertises a trip to somewhere. Oh, this itch today to travel! "If I could only get out to the South Pacific. If I could only go to South America or New Zealand. If I could get somewhere else, maybe I'd be satisfied." My friend, you will never be satisfied except with the Word of God. Nothing else will satisfy you.

An Appeal to the Mind

Will you notice the second temptation. It's psychological. Its appeal is to the mind.

Then the devil, taking Him up on a high mountain, showed Him all the kingdoms of the world in a moment of time. And the devil said to Him, "All this authority I will give You, and their glory; for this has been delivered to me, and I give it to whomever I wish. Therefore, if You will worship before me, all will be Yours." (Luke 4:5–7)

One of the greatest revelations we have in the Word of God is this: Satan has control of the kingdoms of this world. The word that is used here is *oikoumene*, which means "inhabited world," and it's a word that was used for the Roman Empire. Satan took our Lord yonder to a mountain and showed Him that great, vast, rolling Roman Empire—all the way from those cold hills of the highlands of Scotland down to the burning sands of the Sahara Desert, all the way from the pillars of Hercules yonder to the slow-moving Euphrates. Of all those great kingdoms, Satan said, "They're mine. I put them all together, and they're Yours —You can have them." It's Satan's appeal to the mind such as Eve's experience when she looked yonder at that fruit and saw that it was pleasant to the eyes.

What is Satan really saying to our Lord? His implication is this: "You are on the way to the throne, and I know You are going by way of the Cross. I have a detour for You. You can miss the horror of the Cross and come to the throne without the Cross." May I say to you, that is without doubt the most satanic insinuation in the world. This same appeal to the mind has gotten into the pulpits of America today, that we should be intellectual, that we should not preach the death of Christ, that the cross of Christ should not be held up. Yet the most brilliant of them all came yonder to Corinth, the city that boasted of its Greek philosophy. This man Paul, who knew their philosophy better than they knew it, came and said to them:

For I determined not to know anything among you except Jesus Christ and Him crucified. (1 Corinthians 2:2)

And he said:

For the message of the cross is foolishness to those who are perishing. (1 Corinthians 1:18)

But he said, "That's what I preach." And, my friend, if Christ went by way of the Cross because it was necessary, then I'll preach the Cross because it is necessary for your salvation and mine. There's no other way. No other way.

Dr. Edward Judson, the son of Adoniram Judson, who headed up the mission after his father's death, made this observation: "My father suffered greatly in Burma, and as a result there has come into existence all these great missionary agencies of this day." And then he made this remarkable statement: "If you get anything without suffering, it's because somebody else suffered for you. And if you suffer and do not succeed, somebody else will get something because you suffered." Oh, what a glorious, wonderful truth that is. It contradicts the philosophy of Satan: "Miss the Cross; You don't need the Cross—it's not essential. You can come to the throne without the Cross." Our Lord said, and will you notice this:

And Jesus answered and said to him, "Get behind Me, Satan! For it is written, 'You shall

worship the LORD your God, and Him only you shall serve.'" (Luke 4:8)

Oh, Satan left out something. Satan said, "If You will worship me only for a moment, I'll give You the kingdom." Our Lord said in effect, "You left out something. You cannot worship without serving. If I worship you, I'll serve you. And we are to worship God only, and Him only are we to serve."

May I say to you, this is a mistake that even some Christians are making today. They think they can serve God on Sunday, and maybe through certain Christian agencies, but that they can live their own lives to suit themselves. My friend, you cannot do that. It's impossible. Listen to Paul in Romans 6:16:

Do you not know that to whom you present yourselves slaves to obey, you are that one's slaves whom you obey, whether of sin leading to death, or of obedience leading to right-eousness?

Don't you know, my friend, that whomever you obey, whatever livery or uniform you wear, you are the servant of that one? If you are serving sin, then sin is your master. Don't fool yourself.

I stood in front of my office window one day and looked across the street at the California Club. There were about fifteen chauffeurs standing and chatting. Walking very briskly, a man came out of the club. I couldn't hear what he said, but he lifted a finger and spoke something. Immediately one chauffeur withdrew from the crowd, went over and opened the door of the car, and the man got in. Then the chauffeur went around the car, got in the driver's seat, and drove off. So I came to the profound conclusion that he and no one else in the crowd was that man's chauffeur because the one you obey is your master. The others didn't obey him.

My friend, today when you serve sin, sin is your master. Our Lord says you are to worship only God, and Him only are you to serve. You can't worship Him without serving Him. And if you're serving sin you cannot worship God.

Realm of the Spirit

We come to the third area of Satan's attack, which is spiritual. Notice verse 9 in Luke 4.

Then he [Satan] brought Him to Jerusalem, set Him on the pinnacle of the temple, and said to Him, "If You are the Son of God, throw Yourself down from here."

And now listen to the old rascal. He becomes pious; he knows a verse or two of Scripture also.

"For it is written:

**'He shall give His angels charge over you, To keep you,'
and,
'In their hands they shall bear you up, Lest you dash your foot against a stone.'"**
(Luke 4:10, 11)

Satan moves now in the realm of the spirit—actually the realm of faith. "Do the spectacular! Demonstrate that You are the Son of God. Show them! Prove it to them, then they'll accept You, they'll believe You."

Eve looked at the forbidden tree, and the third thing she noticed was that it was designed to make one wise. Apparently she thought, "I'll be a little smarter than I am today by eating the fruit of that tree"—esoteric! "I'll get something that will lift me up"—the pride of life.

May I say to you that Satan can quote Scripture, and it was Shakespeare who said that the devil can quote Scripture for his own purpose. I ordinarily agree with Shakespeare, but he's wrong there. The devil can never quote Scripture for his purpose, but he certainly can misquote it for his purpose, and he did misquote it here. He left out that which was all-important—that is, he didn't fully quote the verse: "He shall give His angels charge over you, to keep you *in all your ways*" (Psalm 91:11, italics added). He left out the final four words. God the Father had a way for His Son, and it was not God's way for Him to throw Himself down from the temple. Oh, one of these days Christ will come in the clouds of glory, but it will be in accordance with the Father's will. Now it is not God's will. Faith is our quietly waiting upon God, doing His will.

You know, friend, for you and for me there are two great dangers today. We always think of unbelief being the great danger. Actually, that's not the only danger. The danger on the other side is presumption. Anyone today who will stick his hand in a sack of rattlesnakes and say "God can keep me from harm" is a fool. He is presuming upon God. Couldn't our Lord Jesus cast Himself down from the temple without harm? He certainly could! Why didn't He? Because He was moving by faith. In other words, Satan was saying, "No longer trust Him. Don't go in all His ways, go in Your own way now."

It's an awful thing to see folks moving in these two directions, unbelief on one hand and presuming upon God on the other. It's frightful today. I no longer listen to anyone who commands God to heal somebody. Who does he think God is, a messenger boy for Western Union? What right has little man to presume upon God and command Him to do anything? Our Lord can keep us in all His ways, and we are to walk in faith, but let's not presume on Him, my beloved. Unbelief is a danger, but presumption is a danger also.

Why Was Jesus Tested?

Jesus was tested, first of all, to demonstrate that we have an impeccable Savior. I have One today in whom I can have utmost confidence. He's able to save to the uttermost. All power, He said, was given to Him in heaven and in earth. I have that kind of Savior. He stood the test.

And second, there is a Man in glory today, at this very moment, who knows me and sympathizes with me. And when I go down through the darkness of this life and come to the battles I must fight and to that place where I cannot win in my own strength, Christ Jesus is there for me, and He knows me; He understands.

Paul has written about this in Hebrews 2:14–18:

> **Inasmuch then as the children have partaken of flesh and blood, He Himself likewise shared in the same, that through death He might destroy him who had the power of death, that is, the devil, and release those who through fear of death were all their lifetime subject to bondage. For indeed He does not give aid to angels, but He does give aid to the seed of Abraham. Therefore, in all things He had to be made like His brethren, that He might be a merciful and faithful High Priest in things pertaining to God, to make propitiation for the sins of the people. For in that He Himself has suffered, being tempted, He is able to aid those who are tempted.**

And then in Hebrews 4:15 and 16 we read:

> **For we do not have a High Priest who cannot sympathize with our weaknesses, but was in all points tempted as we are, yet without sin. Let us therefore come boldly to the throne of grace, that we may obtain mercy and find grace to help in time of need.**

In 1 John 2:1, the apostle John wrote:

> **My little children** [little born ones]**, these things I write to you, so that you may not sin.**

Oh, I wish I were on that spiritual plane. And if
that's all the apostle could say, I would be discour-
aged today. "My little born ones, these things I write
to you, so that you may not sin!" But what if I fail?
Listen,

**And if anyone sins, we have an Advocate with
the Father, Jesus Christ the righteous.**

Oh, when I'm a good boy, it's nice to have someone
pat me on the back. But it's when I'm not good that
I need somebody on my side. "If anyone sins"—He
doesn't turn against us! He doesn't say, "Get Me the
club. Now I'm going to hit him." If anyone sins—at
the time when everybody else turns against us—at
that moment "we have an Advocate with the Father,
Jesus Christ the righteous." He comes in on our
side, and He says, "I am for him. I'm for him because
I know his battle; I know his weakness. I know all
about him. I sympathize with him because I was
down there. And I've undertaken to get him all the
way home to glory. I am able to do it. I didn't fail. I
stood the test. I took the penalty of his sin—he's
Mine. I can save him." How wonderful that I have
an Advocate with the Father, wonderful that when
I need somebody to understand me and to help me,
He's up there for me! My friend, though the whole
world would turn against you today, if you are His,
He's for you. And it is because He went yonder
through the evil darkness of that satanic temptation
on our behalf. Out in the wilderness He faced what

I face and you face. Then He went to the Cross to die a death that you and I cannot go through!

The King of love my Shepherd is
Whose goodness faileth never,
I nothing lack if I am His,
And He is mine forever.

Perverse and foolish, oft I stray,
And yet in love He sought me,
And on His shoulder gently laid
And home rejoicing brought me.

And so through all the length of days,
Thy goodness faileth never.
Good Shepherd, may I sing Thy praise
Within thy house forever.

—Henry W. Baker

CHAPTER 5

WHEN JESUS WENT THROUGH SAMARIA
(JOHN 4)

There is a sense in which the Gospel of John can be classified as the simple Gospel, for it's couched and clothed in simple language. We know it is written for plain people because plain language is used. The grammar is comparatively easy. If I had the privilege of teaching Greek grammar to you for six months, I believe you could read the Gospel of John in Greek at the end of that time. It's filled with monosyllabic words. It has very few polysyllabic words. If you read the first chapter of John with that in mind, you will be amazed how simple the Gospel of John really is as far as the language is concerned.

But in another real sense it's the most profound of all the four Gospels. It's the deepest and the most penetrating. It's beyond the comprehension of the human mind. The thought here is lofty. It is exalted. When I read it I feel like I'm missing something. Although I seem to know what he's saying, I sense there is more. There is something just beyond the fingertips of my spiritual comprehension that I don't quite get. It's out of reach of my childish mind.

I remember in seminary, my last year in a denominational seminary in the East, a lecturer came to give our annual series of lectures. He was known as a profound thinker. After he had spoken three times, I honestly had no notion what he was talking about. I could not understand exactly what he was getting at. So I went to the professor on our faculty who was the man with the highest I.Q. and with more degrees than any other. I said to him, "I thought I was able to get anything that any man would say, but I seem to be missing what Dr. So-and-So is saying." I never shall forget his reply. He said, "Vernon, you know when you're out in the mountains and you come to a pool of water, a cool, clear, limpid pool sixty feet deep, and you can see the bottom of it. But when you're walking down a muddy road and you come to a hoofprint filled with muddy water, you can't see the bottom." Then he said this, "You know, some men are not deep; they are muddy."

May I say to you that John is the opposite of that. He's crystal clear in his language. Because you do see the bottom of the language, you think you're getting it all. But it doesn't mean he's not deep just because you can understand the language.

Now the incident before us is an example of this.

He left Judea and departed again to Galilee.

But He needed to go through Samaria. (John 4:3, 4)

It says here that He needed to go through Samaria. Now that's simple enough. Actually a child can understand that. A sixth-grader could get a map and point out Samaria and explain it all to you with no difficulty whatever. But, oh, my friend, you know there is a sweep here that's breathtaking and awe-inspiring. And I must confess that I don't quite get it.

But He needed to go through Samaria. (John 4:4)

You say, "Well, I understand that." Do you? Let's move back for a moment and get a perspective on what John is saying. He begins:

In the beginning was the Word, and the Word was with God, and the Word was God. (John 1:1)

May I say that this verse moves you farther back in eternity than any other place in the Bible you can go. Genesis 1:1 was fifteen minutes ago compared to John 1:1. John 1:1 goes back into the eternal ages where my little mind and your mind will not be able to comprehend it at all. Out of eternity, the "Word," the Lord Jesus Christ, the expression of God, the communication of God, comes to earth.

Now move down to verse 14, "And the Word became flesh." Literally, He pitches His tent here among us. He is born in Bethlehem and grows up in Nazareth. He has a human body. And I read here, "But He needed to go through Samaria." He *needed to!* The God who came out of eternity past had on His itinerary a trip through Samaria because there is some unknown, forgotten person there with whom the God of all eternity must have an interview. I say to you, I don't quite get that. The God of eternity comes out of eternity and deliberately charts His course through Samaria.

And then I read something else about this One who created the heavens and the earth:

Thus the heavens and the earth, and all the host of them, were finished. And on the seventh day God ended His work which He had done, and He rested on the seventh day from all His work which he had done. (Genesis 2:1, 2)

Notice that it says He rested. He wasn't tired, but He had finished the job. But I read here in John 4:

So He came to a city of Samaria which is called Sychar, near the plot of ground that Jacob gave to his son Joseph. Now Jacob's well was there. Jesus therefore, being wearied from His journey, sat thus by the well. (John 4:5, 6)

The God of eternity came out of eternity, took upon Himself our frail humanity, and with an effort He kept an engagement in Samaria.

He crossed over every barrier that day, racial lines, religious lines, lines that they had set up dividing even men and women. And He crossed over all the lines of the Roman Empire. The God of eternity did all this in order to reach a poor sinner. I say to you, friend, I don't quite get it. But it's tremendous! And it's wonderful and glorious that He would do this in order that He might reach a sinner.

Now will you notice this personal and private interview with the most notorious person yonder in the town. This woman didn't make an appointment. The fact of the matter is the God of eternity had arranged the appointment. She resented His approach. She resisted any effort to bring to her attention anything spiritual. She had no comprehension whatsoever. And I read:

A woman of Samaria came to draw water. Jesus said to her, "Give Me a drink." (John 4:7)

Oh, my friend, today the One who created this universe and the One who created water asked for a drink of it! I thought of this the other day crossing from Victoria over to Port Angeles when the wind was blowing. There's a lot of water there! Out of the eternity of the past into time, taking upon Himself humanity, getting tired at noonday, He sits down on a well and says to the sinner woman, "Give Me a drink." What condescension!

How far down have you and I gone? How far away have we gone? What effort are we making today to reach the unsaved? Haven't our churches really become sort of religious clubs where we eat, drink, and be merry? And we're making no real effort at all to reach the unsaved today.

May I say to you, our Lord left heaven's glory. He crossed over the cultural borderline and asked drink of a woman of Samaria. He did it not because He was thirsty for the water in Jacob's well—I've read this account again carefully, and I don't find that He ever did get His drink out of the well. But He was satisfied. He told the disciples when they returned from town with food and urged Him to eat, "I have food to eat of which you do not know." He was thirsty for her soul and for the souls of those in Samaria. He crossed over the line.

Now I would like to make the introduction of this woman—maybe you don't want to meet her. The women in that day carried the water. That was a very good custom, by the way, women did the work! Early in the morning, before it got hot, the women from the town would come down to the well and draw the water, and again late in the evening when it was cool they'd come down, draw the water, and take it back to their homes. But this woman is down there at noon. Why is she down there at noon? Well, to put it very candidly, she was not popular with the women in the town. The good, respectable women in Samaria didn't care to come down to the well with her. And evidently she didn't care to come down with them. She had been insulted, I suppose, a great many times. So she quit coming except at noon. She did not expect anyone to be there. But when she got there, she found that there was Someone sitting on the well.

Notice how this woman reacted. I'd like for you to get acquainted with her.

Then the woman of Samaria said to Him, "How is it that You, being a Jew, ask a drink from me, a Samaritan woman?" For Jews have no dealings with Samaritans. (John 4:9)

Her reply to Him is rude. It's insolent. It's the kind of answer a woman like this would give.

I wish we had a picture of her, but this is the way I see her. The Lord Jesus had come out of eternity to talk to her and there He sits. She never expected anyone, and she's frightened at first. When she's over the fright she tosses that pert little head of hers, thinking, *Huh, a Jew sitting on the well, and He says give Me a drink!* To Him she says, "How is it that You, being a Jew, ask a drink from me, a Samaritan woman?" She's rubbing it in. Everything she says is insulting. In other words, "What right have You to talk to me? I'm a woman, You're a man; people don't do that here. And You are a Jew. You people think You are superior to us. You won't have any dealings with us Samaritans. We are mongrels to you; we're half-breeds. Why are You asking me for a drink?" And she just tosses her saucy little head and thinks, *Nothing doing. If He thinks I'm going to give Him water, He is wrong.*

Will you listen to our Lord? Oh, friends, how we need to learn from Him. The folks who crudely give out tracts and rudely witness ought to take a lesson from our Lord on witnessing. Will you notice Him?

Jesus answered and said to her, "If you knew the gift of God, and who it is who says to you, 'Give Me a drink,' you would have asked Him, and He would have given you living water." (John 4:10)

Our Lord dealt with this woman skillfully and sympathetically. He dealt with her forcefully and faithfully and factually also. No, He did not give a talk here on integration. He did not give a message on civil rights. He wasn't running for office, as you can see. Oh, we hear so much today that is not helpful. Let's take a lesson from our Lord. Notice His method. He appealed to her womanly curiosity. He created an interest and a thirst.

I read that CocaCola spends more money than any advertiser in the world. Do you know why? To create a thirst. They just come out and say it. If you've been riding down the highway you may have seen their billboard. It has only one word on it, "Thirsty?" If you weren't before, you are then, and you want to know the next place that sells the stuff. May I say to you, that's legitimate. They create a thirst.

Our Lord is creating a thirst in the heart of this Samaritan woman. He says to her—and notice everything is along that line—"If you knew the gift of God, . . . There is something you don't know." And, believe me, if there is something a woman doesn't know, she wants to know! "If you knew who it is asking you for a drink. . . . " Yes, she would like to know who He is. "You would ask Me, and I would give you a different kind of water, the water of life."

Now this woman is beginning to change here. Her attitude is definitely changing. Have you noticed it? "The woman said to Him, 'Sir'. . ." When she first addressed Him after He had asked for a drink, she didn't even say "Sir." But now He's begotten an interest. She is looking at Him in a different light—He's suggesting that He has water to give. She says:

"Sir, You have nothing to draw with, and the well is deep. Where then do You get that living water?" (John 4:11)

She immediately puts the problem to Him. Her thinking is down in the bottom of Jacob's well, and she's talking about that water when she says, "You can't get at it. You have to have a long rope to get it, and You don't even have a container to put it in. How could You give me water?" You see, she's already missed the point. And then in a derogatory way she asks, "Are You greater than our father Jacob?" She claims Jacob for her people, and she has a right to do that. The Samaritans were the off-breed. You see, when Assyria conquered the northern kingdom of Israel and took them into captivity, they left the poor in the land who intermarried with the colonists brought in by the Assyrians. The result was this group called the Samaritans who were present in the land when the Jews came back from captivity. And these half-breeds were not accepted by Israel. The Samaritans were simply ruled out. But notice that this Samaritan woman claims Jacob as her ancestor, and she is accurate. Our Lord never did question that, you see.

> **"Are You greater than our father Jacob, who gave us the well, and drank from it himself, as well as his sons and his livestock?"** (John 4:12)

And as great as old Jacob was, he had to have water out of the well to drink. I don't think our Lord ever got a drink out of this well. He didn't need it. Jacob did, and he drank out of this well.

You see, she's changed her attitude, but she's not getting very high in her thinking. Actually, her thinking is no higher than the water level in the well.

Now will you notice our Lord again. How gracious He is.

> **Jesus answered and said to her, "Whoever drinks of this water will thirst again."** (John 4:13)

The water that's in Jacob's well is H2O, but that's not the water He's dealing with here at all. He's talking about another well because, friends, these wells down here are crowded.

> **"But whoever drinks of the water that I shall give him will never thirst. But the water that**

**I shall give him will become in him a fountain
of water springing up into everlasting life."**
(John 4:14)

We find out later that He is speaking of the Holy
Spirit, whom He gives to those who believe in Him,
but He doesn't say that to the woman. She hasn't
even learned the first lesson yet. She's not very alert
spiritually. She's not interested in any water except
the water in that well. But our Lord says, "That
water that you're getting out of this well won't
satisfy you." And we'll find out in a moment that
she was not satisfied.

Oh, how many folk today are drinking at the
fountains, the poor, broken cisterns of this world
today! They are crowded, and people flock to them;
but they don't find lasting satisfaction, and they
have to keep going back. I heard a man say a while
back, "I've never been drunk like I wanted to be
drunk. I've never had enough." Oh, how many people today are drinking, drinking, drinking! They're
drinking at all sorts of fountains. Because at the
soda fountains of life today, you can get any flavor
you want. You can be entertained, my friend, but
you'll have to go back for more. Our Lord, in effect,
says, "I'm not talking about the fountains of this
world. I'm talking about a spring that will spring up
within *you* so that you not only will never thirst
again, but you'll be able to help others."

Notice Him as He continues to deal with this
woman:

The woman said to Him, "Sir, give me this water, that I may not thirst, nor come here to draw." (John 4:15)

Now she has asked for this water, although obviously she does not clearly understand. You see, at first she says, "Give me this water that I thirst not—the water that I can drink because I'm thirsty." But immediately she takes a dive right back into the well, "And I won't have to come here and draw." She almost got spiritual insight. There was a flash of comprehension for a moment. Our Lord is leading her into the light. She says, "I'd like to have the kind of water You are talking about. I don't like to come here and draw water all the time, especially at noontime."

Notice Jesus' next words:

Jesus said to her, "Go, call your husband, and come here." (John 4:16)

This is the masterstroke. Although the water is available for all, there is a condition to be met— there must be a thirst, a need. She must, therefore, recognize that she is a sinner. So our Lord says to her, "Go, call your husband." He put His finger on the tender spot in her life, "Go, call your husband, and then you come here with him."

Now the woman returns to her flippant manner. Listen to her:

The woman answered and said, "I have no husband." (John 4:17)

She's right back where she started. "I have no husband." She had had too many husbands, and when you have that many, you don't really have any. Poor woman.

Jesus said to her, "You have well said, 'I have no husband,' for you have had five husbands, and the one whom you now have is not your husband; in that you spoke truly." (John 4:17, 18)

She was accurate about that. She had had five husbands, but she didn't have one then. She was living with a man in adultery. Our Lord insists that when you come to Him, you must deal with sin. All secrets must come out before Him. Here was a sinner. One of the reasons she was not so popular with the women of the town was because she was too popular with the men of the town.

The woman said to Him, "Sir, I perceive that You are a prophet." (John 4:19)

She is shocked into reverence, and now she addresses Him respectfully as "Sir." She's moving forward now. Oh, she's learning the first lesson, which is, "The fear of the LORD is the beginning of wisdom," (Proverbs 9:10). In the life she has led, she has had no fear of God or man. When you come to Jesus, you must come as the sinner you are. That's the way she will have to come.

Although she is startled into fear, she does a popular thing that folk still do today.

"Our fathers worshiped on this mountain, and you Jews say that in Jerusalem is the place where one ought to worship." (John 4:20)

Isn't that interesting? Here is a woman who is practically a prostitute, and she wants to argue about where to worship God. Many people want to sidestep reality and raise a religious question. It's amazing the number of people who say, "Well, I just can't believe the story about Jonah." You can't? What's the trouble? "Well, I don't think a man could live for three days and three nights in the belly of a fish." Isn't your problem really that *you're* having trouble living? It's not Jonah that you have a problem with; it's yourself.

Oh, how many people today want to argue religion who are not prepared to live it! I'm convinced that most of the superficiality in our churches today— they are honeycombed with hypocrisy—is because there has been a definite compromise with evil. Even professing Christians will not face up to sin. They do not object to the pastor preaching on the sins of the Moabites which were committed four thousand years ago, but they don't want to hear about their sins here in our contemporary culture!

There are many preachers today, and I know this to be a fact, who are afraid to preach on the sins of Christians. This has been confirmed in my own thinking recently. It has been my custom when I go to summer conferences to use a series of messages and repeat the same series throughout the summer season. By the time I've come to the last conference,

I know a little something of what I'm talking about. Well, this year it was the Epistle to the Romans, and I learned to watch the reactions. The first day especially there was resentment because the first day I always spoke on sin. The second day I spoke on the fact that everybody is a sinner, including the man sitting in the pew, the deacon, the elder, and the preacher. We all are sinners in God's sight. By that time I felt like I ought to leave. I was probably the most unpopular man there. But by the middle of the week there was a breaking up and melting down so that by the end of the conference the Holy Spirit was really working.

In one conference a very pompous and pious saint came to me at the beginning to tell me that he was a preacher's son and that from the time he was a little fellow he had been in the church. He had grown up in the church. He was active in the church. He was a big man in his church, and he wanted me to know it. Also, he wanted to tell me what he thought about some others. At the end of the conference—I never shall forget it—he came to me, tears streaming down his face. He said, "Dr. McGee, I want to talk with you. Do you really think I ought to continue on in the position I have in the church? I have seen myself for the first time."

In another conference two preachers wanted an interview. And do you know what their question was? They said, "Do you preach like this in your own pulpit?" I said, "Well, I never change my message. We have two or three members of my church here, and you can go ask them."

They said, "How do you get by with it? Don't you get in trouble?" I said, "Yes, I do. Frankly, God has given me a wonderful church, some of the most wonderful people. No preacher in this day of Laodicea should be ungrateful when 2,500 people come out to midweek Bible study. How I was humbled by that. But in the congregation there's a little cell of members who do for me, the preacher, what they try to do for you—crucify me! They criticize the preacher so that they can divert attention from themselves because they know they're rotten within. But they don't want to face up to it. There's a psychological problem involved when you begin to criticize somebody else to take attention off yourself." And then I asked them this, "Have you ever noticed that when you throw a rock at a bunch of dogs, it's always the hit dog that hollers?"

Now our Lord did not avoid the religious issue. This woman—well, I don't think she has asked an honest question yet, and I personally would not have been as gracious as my Lord was here—He took time out to answer her. I would have said, "Wait a minute, let's stick to the subject. I want to talk about those five husbands and this bird you're living with now." Our Lord didn't. How gracious He was! She said, "I wonder where we should worship, in this mountain or in Jerusalem? Would You tell me where to worship?" You know, friends, if we are honest in our questions, Jesus will always answer us.

Jesus said to her, "Woman, believe Me, the

hour is coming when you will neither on this mountain, nor in Jerusalem, worship the Father." (John 4:21)

In other words, "Actually the question that you raised is irrelevant; it's not pertinent at all. It's not *where* you worship. It's *Who* you worship and *how* you worship that's important."

"You worship what you do not know; we know what we worship, for salvation is of the Jews." (John 4:22)

Why did He say, "for salvation is of the Jews"? There are several reasons, of course, but this is one that maybe you had not noticed. She said, "How is it that You, being a Jew, ask a drink from me, a Samaritan woman?" He is going to let her know that He Himself is the Savior. Notice His syllogistic reasoning: "You call me a Jew. Salvation is of the Jews. I am a Jew." My friend, don't say He was not a Jew—He was a Jew in the days of His flesh.

"But the hour is coming, and now is, when the true worshipers will worship the Father in spirit and truth; for the Father is seeking such to worship Him. God is Spirit, and those who worship Him must worship in spirit and truth." (John 4:23, 24)

Now this woman's heart is opened. May I say to you, she's profoundly interested now. And wistfully, with a longing in her heart, she responds to Him.

Here's a woman who is a well-known sinner. The good women of Samaria would have nothing to do with her, but they didn't know her heart. Our Lord did, and down beneath her sin there is a spiritual longing. Listen to her:

The woman said to Him, "I know that Messiah is coming" (who is called Christ). "When He comes, He will tell us all things." (John 4:25)

In all of her sins, she was looking for the Messiah. Isn't that amazing? Listen to this woman, "I know that Messiah is coming." (It is as if she is saying, "Oh, if He'd only come now!") "When He comes, He will tell us all things." She is ready now for the most glorious transaction any soul can have.

This is the most majestic and sublime thing our Lord has said. Listen to Him:

Jesus said to her, "I who speak to you am He." (John 4:26)

Isn't that glorious? In other words, "I am the Messiah! Woman, I knew in the eternal ages of the past that you would be looking for the Messiah. I knew that you would be a sinner. I've come to save sinners, and in God's eternal Book I wrote down an appointment with you to come through Samaria just to tell you, *He is here, He is here.* I am the Messiah."

My friend, have you had that wonderful transaction with Christ, when He said to you, "I am He, I'm the One to meet the need of your heart"? Has it been personal? Has it been real?

If you want to know how genuine she was, notice what she did:

The woman then left her waterpot, went her way into the city, and said to the men, "Come, see a Man who told me all things that I ever did. Could this be the Christ?" (John 4:28, 29)

No woman would have listened to her, but the men all knew her. And several men responded. Oh, they snapped to attention, "You mean to tell me He knows everything you've done? If He knows about you, He knows about me." And we're told that the men of the town came to Him.

And many of the Samaritans of that city believed in Him because of the word of the woman who testified, "He told me all that I ever did." (John 4:39)

Our Lord reached Samaria through a woman with a shady past. But she was looking for Someone, the Messiah, to take away her sins. She was really thirsty, not primarily for that water in the well, but for the Water of Life.

I conclude with the last invitation of the Bible:

And the Spirit and the bride say, "Come!" And let him who hears say, "Come!" And let him who thirsts come. Whoever desires, let

him take the water of life freely. (Revelation 22:17)

Are you thirsty? He's thirsty for you if you are thirsty for Him. He died for you, and when you come it satisfies His soul. "He shall see the labor of His soul, and be satisfied. . . . for He shall bear their iniquities" (Isaiah 53:11).

CHAPTER 6

WHEN JESUS MET A DAD
AND HIS LAD
(MARK 9:2–29)

Before us now is one of the greatest miracles
recorded in the Word of God. It is the healing of a
lad who was demon possessed. We'll let Mark paint
this picture for us. It is a remarkable picture that is
bigger than this little world on which we live—it
encompasses time and space.

**Now after six days Jesus took Peter, James,
and John, and led them up on a high mountain apart by themselves; and He was trans-
figured before them.** (Mark 9:2)

Jesus took with Him yonder to the mountain three
of His disciples, leaving the other nine below. He
went up there to pray, and while He was praying the
Transfiguration took place.

**His clothes became shining, exceedingly
white, like snow, such as no launderer on
earth can whiten them. And Elijah appeared**

> to them with Moses, and they were talking with Jesus. Then Peter answered and said to Jesus, "Rabbi, it is good for us to be here; and let us make three tabernacles: one for You, one for Moses, and one for Elijah"—because he did not know what to say, for they were greatly afraid. And a cloud came and over-shadowed them; and a voice came out of the cloud, saying, "This is My beloved Son. Hear Him!" (Mark 9:3–7)

Jesus was glorified, transfigured, and as you look at Him there, you see God's goal for humanity. God's intention for you and me is what you find there on the Mount of Transfiguration! While He was trans-figured, Moses and Elijah appeared with Him. Peter, James, and John were also with Him there on the Mount.

Now let's come down from the mountain. At the foot of the mountain there is a scene of tragedy. Frankly, I think it's one of the worst scenes we have in the entire Word of God. A father has brought his son, and the boy is demon possessed. Not only is it the worst case you'll find, it is also the most pitiful, the most hopeless case. Humanly speaking, the boy is incurable.

Added to that is a scene of defeat and humiliation for the nine disciples, for that father brought his son to the disciples since Jesus was not there, and they could do nothing for him. Yes, it was a scene of defeat and humiliation. And worse still, there's a crowd there watching the sad spectacle and wonder-ing. They are skeptical now of the power of Jesus.

And the enemy, in the form of the scribes, is there to gloat, to jeer, to ridicule and criticize. That's the picture.

Notice the contrast. Yonder on the mountain our Lord was glorified. That was God's goal for humanity. That is God's ideal and intention for mankind, and that is the place to which He will bring His own someday, for we do not know how we shall appear, but according to 1 John 3:2, we know that when He shall appear, we shall be like Him!

Down at the foot of that mountain there is a demon-possessed boy, the product of sin, and I could only wish that Father Adam could be there for a moment and see what it meant to disobey God as he did and what sin really was—look at the boy. Now look at the whole picture: Jesus glorified on the mountain! At the foot of the mountain the demon-possessed boy! That's what sin can do for you. Mark has sketched this scene for us.

But in this world where you and I live at the foot of the mountain, we are like those helpless disciples at the foot of the mount, in the presence of a demon-possessed world. You can't look out on this world today, my friend, without seeing that this restless world, where there are literal and political earthquakes taking place everywhere, is demon possessed. And in this sad hour the church is helpless and hopeless, making no impact upon our world. Seemingly, we can do nothing. What a picture!

With that as a background, I'd like to focus our attention on this father and his demon-possessed boy, a dad and his lad, and how our Lord took charge of the situation. Our Lord came down from the mountain, from that celestial air—oh, it was heady up there. But He came down. Peter had said, "Let's stay here and build some tabernacles." Our Lord had said, in substance, "There's no use building tabernacles while men are demon possessed, while there is such a desperate need below." So He came down.

And when He came to the disciples, He saw a great multitude around them, and scribes disputing with them. (Mark 9:14)

He came to the disciples who had failed to heal the boy and to that curious mob watching, with nothing else to do. The scribes are adding to the chagrin and the embarrassment of the disciples. Our Lord immediately comes to the side of His disciples and defends them. He turns to the scribes and says to them, "You have some questions you're putting to My disciples? You put them to Me. I'll answer them." But the interesting thing is that the scribes have had encounters with our Lord before and have never yet come off the winner, so they don't open their mouths.

But out of that faceless mob walks a man, a father, and he's the only one identified in that crowd of people. Will you listen to him:

Then one of the crowd answered and said, "Teacher, I brought You my son, who has a mute spirit." (Mark 9:17)

You see, the scribes had said nothing, so this father steps out and in effect says, "I'm sorry. I'm the cause of all the commotion and all the embarrassment. I brought my boy to You."

Now the father is before us. In Dr. Luke's account, he adds a tender touch here. The man further says, "He is my only child"—the only son of the father, demon possessed! That is the tragic picture.

Three features stand out in this encounter. In fact, out of the context there are three inescapable and self-evident truths. First, there is the responsibility of the father; second, the recognition of the desperate case of the boy; third, there is the realization that Jesus is his only hope.

(Somebody asked me the other day, "Why is it that you always find *three* things to build your messages around? Why don't you find two or four?" I'll tell you why, in case you have wondered. I always lift out three points because two are not enough and four are too many!)

Responsibility of the Father

First of all, look with me at the responsibility of the father. There is no need of laboring to establish this point. I think it's obvious. This father took time out to bring his son to Christ. He came in anguish; he's almost beside himself. And our Lord asks this father, "How long has this been happening to him?" And he says, "From childhood."

There are always some questions that crop up in your mind when you read that. Had the father neglected the son when he was a little lad so that he's in this condition? Did it take a tragedy to alert this father to his responsibility? Had he really waited too long before he took an interest in the boy? I do not know, and I'll not speculate. I *do* know that at this time the father assumed full responsibility. Now, I'm willing to go along and say that out yonder on the fringe of the crowd stands an anxious mother. She's out there somewhere, I feel sure of that, but it's the father who brings the child to Jesus. The same is true of the little girl who died. In chapter 5 of Mark we read that the mother stayed with the little girl while the father came to get Jesus. I do not know the background of either situation. I only know that this father now assumes full responsibility for the boy. "He's my boy; he's demon possessed, and I'm bringing him to You." Oh, he probably lost a day's wages, but he would have taken off work for a month if necessary.

In the past few years a great deal has been made of Father's Day. You've probably noticed that the merchants have taken advantage of it. I do suspect that they have ulterior motives. I think they're more interested in honoring father's check than in honoring father and more interested in making a grand than in the grand old man. They're more interested in dough than dad and in profits than pater. But nevertheless, father is getting recognition. And it does afford an opportunity to call attention to the biblical responsibility of a father.

Now for years mothers have assumed responsibility for rearing the children. You and I have been brought up in a society where the spiritual leadership in the home has been taken too often by the mother. I want to say today that this is becoming passé—not because fathers have moved back into the home and are taking their responsibility, but because mothers have joined them down at the local bar. Society is now placing the responsibility on the church, on the school, and on society itself for the child's failure. And he is failing, don't forget. Now today the sociologists are placing the blame on the educational system, on law enforcement officials and regulations, and on the breakdown of the American homes. And then there are others who are saying that spiritual leadership is the church's job. I disagree with that. It's not the church's job. The spiritual life of a boy is the responsibility of his dad. And a dad needs to get very close to his boy.

Oh, I do not mean to give him the facts of life; he already knows those. The story is told of a father who said to his son, "Son, I want to talk to you about the facts of life." The boy said, "Okay, Dad, what do you want to know?"

May I say to you again that it's the responsibility of the father to lead his own son to a saving knowledge of Christ. And he'll have to get very close to him if he is going to do the job. And believe me, friends, the most wonderful thing a father can possibly do is to lead his boy to the Lord.

What is a boy? I like Alan Beck's description, sent to me by a listener. It is titled, "What Is a Boy?" Let me share it with you.

Between the innocence of babyhood and the dignity of manhood we find a delightful creature called a boy. . . . Boys are found everywhere—on top of, underneath, inside of, climbing on, swinging from, running around, or jumping to. Mothers love them, little girls hate them, older sisters and brothers tolerate them, adults ignore them, and Heaven protects them. A boy is Truth with dirt on its face, Beauty with a cut on its finger, Wisdom with bubble gum in its hair, and the Hope of the future with a frog in its pocket.

When you are busy, a boy is an inconsiderate, bothersome, intruding jangle of noise. When you want him to make a good impression, his brain turns to jelly or else he becomes a savage, sadistic, jungle creature bent on destroying the world and himself with it.

A boy is a composite—he has the appetite of a horse, the digestion of a sword swallower, the energy of a pocket-size atomic bomb, the curiosity of a cat, the lungs of a dictator, the imagination of a Paul Bunyan, the shyness of a violet, the audacity of a steel trap, the enthusiasm of a firecracker, and when he makes something, he has five thumbs on each hand. . . .

Nobody else gets so much fun out of trees, dogs, and breezes. Nobody else can cram into one pocket a rusty knife, a half-eaten apple, three feet of string, an empty Bull Durham sack, two gumdrops, six cents, a slingshot, a chunk of unknown substance, and a genuine supersonic code ring with a secret compartment.

A boy is a magical creature—you can lock him out of your workshop, but you can't lock him out of your heart. You can get him out of your study, but you can't get him out of your mind. Might as well give up—he is your captor, your jailer, your boss, and your master—a freckled-faced, cat-chasing, bundle of noise. But when you come home at night with only the shattered pieces of your hopes and dreams, he can mend them like new with the two magic words — "Hi, Dad!"

And let's not forget that it is the dad's responsibility to get his lad to Christ. Have you done that?

Recognition of the Lad's Desperate Case

Then one of the crowd answered and said, "Teacher, I brought You my son, who has a mute spirit. And wherever it seizes him, it throws him down; he foams at the mouth, gnashes his teeth, and becomes rigid. So I spoke to Your disciples, that they should cast it out, but they could not.... And often he has thrown him both into the fire and into the water to destroy him. But if You can do anything, have compassion on us and help us." (Mark 9:17, 18, 22)

Demon possession is the worst malady that can happen to any member of the human family. And when a child is sick, especially with a fatal disease, it's far more critical and terrible than when an adult gets the same disease and is in the same condition. I say to you, because he is a boy and because of the fact that he is demon possessed, he is the worst case in Scripture. This distraught father made no attempt to conceal it. He didn't attempt to somehow camouflage or state the true case in other terms. He didn't deny the condition of the boy.

In my opinion the saddest condition of Christian parents today is that they think they're raising little angels when they're raising big brats. A great many Christian parents today will not recognize that their child has a need, and a desperate need. They will not acknowledge that he's a little sinner before God and needs to be saved.

A mother was having trouble with her boy, so she went to a psychiatrist for counsel. The psychiatrist asked her some questions, and one of them was, "Does he have a feeling of insecurity?" She looked puzzled for a moment, then said, "No, I don't think he has a feeling of insecurity, but everybody in the neighborhood does."

A Bible school teacher in a church I pastored came to me and said, "I don't know what to do. I have a problem child in my class, so I went to the father, and he denied everything. He said, 'My boy cannot nor would he ever tell a lie. He always tells the truth.'" I wonder if that father knows that the Lord Jesus said:

For out of the heart proceed evil thoughts, murders, adulteries, fornications, thefts, false witness, blasphemies. (Matthew 15:19)

One of those is false witness. It is the tendency and bent of a fallen nature to lie. You don't have to teach anybody to lie—they lie naturally. You have to teach them to tell the truth. The father went on to say, "And my boy has never said a bad word." Probably he has not read what Paul wrote in Romans 3:14, "Whose mouth is full of cursing and bitterness."

There have been many parents, Christian parents, who have lost their children as they've grown up. They had veneered them nicely. The fact of the matter is, some of them put their children in a plastic bag, saying, "My little Willie or my little Suzie is separated." Separated from what? May I ask you, have you ever led them to a saving knowledge of Christ? Have they been born again? Have they been given a new nature in Christ? Unless they have a new nature, they will lie and they will cuss.

When I came to the church I pastored in Los Angeles, a man who was then a church officer told me about his grown children. He said, "My children, I'm thankful, are all saved." They were not with him in our services but had gone out to other churches, liberal churches. And I've been told that their lives are no different from those of the non-Christian, and yet their father will defend them. I say to you today, my friend, we need to recognize the desperate condition of a lost heart, and that lost heart can be that little lad who is in your home. Until he's been born again he is a lost sinner. He needs to be instructed and disciplined. Oh, I know that we don't want to be harsh.

I love this little poem and pass it on to you:

I spanked a little boy last night.
   I thought I was doing right.
I thought that I was punishing
   a little boy for some wrong thing.
Today I bought a ball and kite
   for that same boy I spanked last night.
Bought marbles, tops, and everything
   to counteract the punishing.
You see, through tears this little lad
   tried hard to smile, then said, "Dad,
Will spanking make me good like you?"
   I think you would have bought things too.

Yes, I think discipline should be administered very carefully by sinful parents, although it does need to be administered. Oh, we need to recognize that our children's basic problem is that they are lost until they have come to Christ. And let's not just put a little veneer around them or slip them into a plastic bag and say, "My little Willie is saved because he can quote John 3:16, and he prays the loveliest little prayer." That's all well and good, but you ought to hear him on the schoolground, and you ought to see what he writes in the latrine.

Oh, my friend, there is today a great need for a recognition of the desperate condition of our little lads.

The Realization That Jesus Was His Only Hope

This poor father felt like the disciples did when our Lord asked them if they were going to leave Him as others had, and they said, "To whom shall we go?

You have the words of eternal life" (John 6:68). But this father was shaken when he first came, and he had a right to be shaken. He said, "Teacher, I brought You my son, who has a mute spirit. . . . So I spoke to Your disciples, that they should cast it out, but they could not." In other words, "I came here with high hopes, great expectancy, and I thought something would be done for my boy, but nothing was done." Listen to Jesus now that He has come down from the mountain and the father has come directly to Him. Our Lord says, "Bring him to Me." And the father brings him. Then the Lord Jesus asks, "How long has this been happening to him?" And the father says, "Often he has thrown him both into the fire and into the water to destroy him." Now listen to him. Listen to this dad's heart cry, "But if You can do anything, have compassion on us and help us." That father had suffered with his son. What touched that boy touched him. His life was wrapped up in that boy. He was pleading for help. "Help us!" And that poor father needed help too, as we shall see. Notice that he said, "If You can do anything"—now don't blame him for saying that. After all, the disciples of Jesus had failed. He's been disappointed. And after all, he has heard the scribes ridiculing Jesus and criticizing Him. Criticism will dilute the work of the Spirit. So he wasn't sure. "I came here. I thought I would get help. If You can do anything—even just a little—have compassion on us and help us!"

Notice the answer of our Lord:

Jesus said to him, "If you can believe, all things are possible to him who believes." (Mark 9:23)

This to me is one of the most wonderful verses in the Scriptures. Jesus said to him, "If you can believe"—but the word *believe* does not appear in our better manuscripts. It was put there by the translators to smooth it out. It does smooth it out, no question, but it makes us miss the point. The answer of Jesus should read: "If you can, all things are possible to him who believes." In order to try to get a correct translation of this verse, I suppose I've examined fifteen translations. When I checked the Revised Standard Version, thinking that here was their opportunity to really show their scholarship, there was none. An IBM machine would have done it the same way.

Now I admit this is a difficult passage of Scripture so we must have somebody to interpret, and I hope somehow or other I can get over to you the meaning of what our Lord said. It's the most wonderful thing in the world. In the Greek text the word for *you* begins the sentence. Maybe that doesn't mean anything to you, so let me say it this way: "You, if *you* can—all things are possible to him who believes."

Will you notice something important here? Our Lord, seizing on this father's cry for help, said in substance, "The thing that interests Me is you. If you can, I can." And if you want to smooth it all the way out, Dr. M. R. Vincent gives this, "If thou canst, all things can be"—if *you* can. You see, friend, our

Lord is limited by the father's lack of faith. That's the only thing in the world that can limit God—lack of faith. And the interesting thing is that the father had caught the point. Oh, this father understood what our Lord was saying, and "immediately the father of the child cried out and said with tears, 'Lord, I believe; help my unbelief.'" The boy is demon possessed and the father doesn't have faith.

"If you can." The "if" belongs to you, brother; if you can believe, the child can be healed. This father knew he was weak, and he knew that he was as sick as his boy was. Our Lord had to bring him to belief in Christ. Jesus is saying, "The *if* is not with Me; the *if* is with you. If you can believe, I can heal your son." And the father says, "I believe You"—then he looks at that poor, helpless, incurable boy and cries, "Oh, help my unbelief!" And, my friend, the minute that father was cured, the son was cured. Isn't that wonderful? The minute the father came into faith in Christ, his boy was cured. You see, the Bible doesn't say that we have juvenile delinquency. The trouble is with the parent. Jesus met the need of that father, and the father believed; when he did, the boy was healed. Someone has said, "Train up a child in the way he should go—and go that way yourself!" The father did this. He came in faith to Christ.

I close with this. I heard Dr. George Truett, who was called the prince of the pulpit, tell a story concerning a lawyer friend of his who later became a judge in Dallas, Texas. He and this lawyer had been friends for awhile. But when he began to push the claims of Christ upon the lawyer, it actually antagonized him, and he would no longer attend the church services. The lawyer married, and his family attended the church. The boy in the family, an only son, kept getting into a little trouble, a little difficulty. One day Dr. Truett talked with the boy together with some others, and the fellow said this, "I know I ought to take Christ as my Savior. I need Him; I know it." Then after thinking a moment he said, "But I like my dad, and everything my dad does is right, and I want to be just like him. He doesn't need Christ, and I don't need Christ either." Dr. Truett said no more to the boy. He went out of his study, walked into downtown Dallas, climbed up two or three flights of steps, came to the office of this lawyer, and went in. The lawyer saw him and said, "Look, if you have come here to talk to me about my soul again, I'm not interested." Dr. Truett said, "I'm not even concerned today to talk to you about your soul. I've come to talk to you about your boy." The man showed some interest then because that boy was the apple of his eye. He said, "Come in and sit down. Is he in trouble again?" Dr. Truett said, "No, he's not, but he's going to get in trouble. I think I ought to tell you about my interview with him. I asked him to accept Christ as his Savior, and he told me he thought he ought to. In fact, he said he thought he needed Christ, but that he liked his dad, and everything his dad did was right. Then he said, 'My dad doesn't need Christ, and I don't need Him either.'" Dr. Truett added, "I think you ought to know that." And in the dignified manner Dr.

Truett was capable of, he said, "I bid you good day." And he walked out of the office and left that man thinking.

The next Sunday morning Dr. Truett looked out over his congregation, and there was the father of the boy. When the invitation was given, he was the first one who responded. Dr. Truett was amazed, then he looked to see where the boy was. While he was looking, he glanced down and the boy was at the altar by the time the father got there. When Dr. Truett went down to speak to them, the father said, "I really didn't know that I needed Jesus so badly."

You see, beloved, many times the fate of the son lies in the faith of the father.

. . . Lord, I believe; help my unbelief!

CHAPTER 7

WHEN JESUS WENT OUT TO DINNER
(LUKE 7:36–50)

**"For John the Baptist came neither eating
bread nor drinking wine, and you say, 'He has
a demon.' The Son of Man has come eating
and drinking, and you say, 'Look, a glutton
and a winebibber, a friend of tax collectors
and sinners!'"** (Luke 7:33, 34)

T he Lord Jesus had a reputation. He was subjected to criticism, of course, and the awful criticism of being called a gluttonous person and a winebibber because He went out to eat so often. What a contrast to John! And our Lord Himself made the contrast. John was an austere man. The Lord Jesus was friendly. John was severe; Jesus was social. John was a solitary individual; the Lord Jesus was gregarious, constantly with people.

Dr. Luke in his Gospel gives us the record of two occasions when the Pharisees invited Jesus out to dinner, and it was always an exciting evening when He went out to dinner because He was the after-dinner speaker. He always did or said something unusual. But believe me, when He went into the home of a Pharisee, it was more unusual. In this message we'll be looking at one of those occasions when He went to the home of a Pharisee, the home of Simon the Pharisee.

Now on the surface, it seemed to be friendly enough. Notice this:

Then one of the Pharisees asked Him to eat with him. And He went to the Pharisee's house, and sat down to eat. (Luke 7:36)

That seems friendly enough, does it not? But on closer examination, which we shall do a little later, we will see there was a lack of cordiality. In fact, there was an open display of hostility and animosity to our Lord on the part of Simon the Pharisee.

Simon actually was insulting to the Lord, and He reminded him of it. It was the common custom in that day to provide water at the door to wash the feet of the guest. Simon had omitted this amenity. May I say to you, he was positively rude in so doing. Also, it was the custom for the host to greet the guest with a kiss. This Pharisee didn't do that. It was also the custom of the day for the host to provide oil for the head of the guest when he came in. Simon had deliberately omitted these common courtesies, which evidenced the hostility of this Pharisee toward our Lord, and the events that followed bear it out.

The question, of course, arises as to why this Pharisee invited the Lord Jesus in the first place. There have been many suggestions. I'll not attempt to mention them, because in my judgment this one alone is satisfactory: The Pharisee sought an opportunity to accuse the Lord Jesus. This was a deliberate attempt to find some charge that could be made against our Lord.

May I say to you, this is without doubt one of the worst breaches of common courtesy imaginable! An invitation to dinner is always considered a token of friendship, a display of warmth and intimacy. When you go into the home of the host, you are under his protection. He should not only shield you from harm, he should shield you from every form of criticism. He is your friend. If it is otherwise, it becomes an awful betrayal.

So this Pharisee had invited the Lord Jesus, but he invited Him, not to be friendly, but to seek something by which he could make a charge against Him, and he wanted to find fault with Him.

Now the next question arises: Why did our Lord go? Would you accept an invitation like this into the home of one you knew was not your friend? Would you go if you knew you were going to be laid open to every form of criticism? Yet our Lord went. He wanted to win that hard, cold, calculating, critical Pharisee as much as He wanted to win that woman who was a sinner (see Luke 7:37). The Pharisee's home that He went into was as unattractive to Christ as the brothel out of which she had come. And our Lord would have been as much at home in that brothel as He was in the home of the Pharisee. But don't be disturbed by that. He left heaven's glory and came down to an unfriendly world, a world that crucified Him. And He came down because He wanted to save.

So it is that our Lord goes into the home of this Pharisee to try to win him. And I think He did, although I have no basis for that other than the events that unfold. Will you follow them with me?

Look for a moment at our host, Simon the Pharisee. Actually, I think he's probably one of the most unattractive fellows you could possibly meet. I don't think I would want to go to his home for dinner. The word *Pharisee* is not a Greek word; it is a Hebrew word. It means "separate." They were a separated crowd, let me tell you! They were a group that rose up in Israel in what is known as the Intertestament Period, between Malachi and the New Testament.

During the Maccabean Period, when Israel was so pressed by Syria in the north and such awful things were happening to them, these men were raised up, loyal to God and loyal to the nation. Like so many organizations that start off well, but after a certain length of time they run down, this organization had run down. It was no longer the vibrant and vital thing it should have been for God. It was made up of men who were self–satisfied and concerned with externals—ceremonies, rituals, washings, and that sort of thing—and when they practiced them, they were saying, "We are better than you."

It was a Pharisee who said in his prayer to God, "I give tithes of all I possess, and I thank You, God, that I'm not like other men or like that publican over there." You never met such a self-satisfied, self-conceited, self-sufficient lot. And this man is marked through the entire meal by self-complacency and a smugness that is almost intolerable. This was Simon the Pharisee. He needed nothing from Jesus, and he wanted nothing from Jesus. He was religious. Oh, there are so many folk like that in our day also!

Now at this dinner one of the most startling episodes imaginable took place:

And behold, a woman in the city who was a sinner, when she knew that Jesus sat at the table in the Pharisee's house, brought an alabaster flask of fragrant oil. (Luke 7:37)

This woman came to that dinner uninvited. She was a sinner. Actually the word that is used—you can't mistake it—says that she was "devoted" to sin. She was notorious; she was infamous; she was a woman of the town, we're told, a woman off the streets. She was a harlot. Notice that the Word of God is very careful to protect such women. Their names are not given. I feel sorry for the preacher who years ago identified this woman with Mary Magdalene. It was two altogether different dinners. But he made the mistake, and since then a great many have tried to identify her as Mary Magdalene. It is not true. She is unidentified. The Spirit of God has protected her.

Now why did this woman of questionable character come in to this dinner? Edersheim, who in many ways was such a great scholar and so enlightening in things that he said, makes an awful statement here. He suggests that Simon had had illicit relationships with her. May I say to you, you can rule that out immediately. Simon the Pharisee would have crossed the street had he seen her coming rather than meet her. He wouldn't have touched her with a twenty-foot pole. This Simon the Pharisee would have had nothing to do with her.

Why did she come? Will you notice something? There was an Eastern custom in that day that when a prominent person in town gave a dinner, the neighbors were free to come in and stand around the wall. In fact, in some places seats were provided for them. All sorts of people would come in during a meal—the curious, the beggars, and some others would come in on business. If a man of prominence gave a dinner, the neighbors might come in, look it over, and say, "Well, you served chicken last time, and I see you have pot roast this time." Or a beggar would come in and say, "I'm hungry. Would you give me something?" Or some man would come in on business and say, "I've been trying to get you all day. I knew I'd find you at home now because I heard you were giving a dinner here tonight. Now I want to buy those twenty head of sheep," and right there and then he would conduct the business transaction. When the man would leave, the dinner would go on. So during the course of an evening, a great crowd of people could have trooped in and out. By the time they got to dessert, there would be a pretty good crowd of spectators—they wouldn't eat however. They were not guests; they were standing on the sidelines.

Now that explains how the woman got in, but it doesn't explain why she got in, does it? Why did she come? Dr. Luke is very careful to give her motive. Look at this again. "When she knew that Jesus sat at the table in the Pharisee's house, [she] brought an alabaster flask of fragrant oil." The explanation is that when she knew *Jesus* was in the house she came. She would never have come under any other circumstances. And, friend, she did one of the love-liest things you'll find in the Word of God:

And [she] stood at His feet behind Him weep-ing; and she began to wash His feet with her tears, and wiped them with the hair of her head; and she kissed His feet and anointed them with the fragrant oil. (Luke 7:38)

Dr. Luke records this with exquisite delicacy. Again let me say that I think it is the loveliest thing that happened to our Lord—this incident and when Mary of Bethany did the same thing right before Christ's death.

Then we have another ancient custom, an East-ern custom that we need to observe. In that day they did not sit in chairs around a table. When I was in Sunday school they gave out cards with biblical scenes to the little folks. I never heard a thing a Sunday school teacher ever said to me, but I sure remember those little cards. And I can still see that picture of Jesus there and Simon sitting across from

Him at our type of table, and the woman was down under the table! Many of those pictures were wrong, and if they still use them, they ought to correct them. This little card was wrong, because in that day they had couches instead of chairs around the table, and they reclined during the meal. The guests had taken off their sandals, and their feet were down at the lower end of the couch. The woman was standing at the back with the other onlookers, directly behind where Jesus was reclining. That is the picture before us, and it helps us to understand what's taking place.

This woman had been a moral leper. She had lived a life of shame, and under the Mosaic Law a harlot was to be stoned. She was in the same class as a publican in that there was no salvation for her. When a man became a publican, he could never again come to the temple and offer sacrifice, and that's what the poor publican was asking God for when he prayed, "O God, be merciful" or literally, "Make a mercy seat for me, a publican, to go to." This poor harlot had no place to go. She was shut out from God, and the Law said, "Stone her." Somewhere out yonder in the city or on the byway or the highway, she had been in a crowd who heard Jesus speaking. Do you want to know some of the things He had already said? "The Son of Man has power on earth to forgive sins" (Luke 5:24). "Come to Me, all you who labor and are heavy laden, and I will give you rest" (Matthew 11:28)—that is, "If you have a burden of sin, come to Me." It was right after the incident of the harlot being dragged before Jesus that He gave this warning: "Therefore I said to you that you will die in your sins; for if you do not believe that I am He, you will die in your sins" (John 8:24). She had believed and had experienced forgiveness of sins. Christ had redeemed her, and due to that fact, He's going to the Cross to suffer the penalty of death for her sins. He had cleansed her. He not only treated her like a lady, He made her a lady! The world condemned her, but Christ forgave her, and now she wants to do something for the One who has done so much for her.

This woman had a very expensive alabaster flask of fragrant oil. She had made money in her profession, and she has something valuable. When she hears that Jesus is reclining at a meal in the Pharisee's home, she breaks down all tradition and determines to go and wait for the opportunity of putting that expensive oil on Him just to let Him know how much she appreciates that her sins are forgiven. So she takes up her silent vigil. Our Lord comes in, and she quietly works her way to the place where He is reclining, then she stands at His feet. This is her opportunity to do this lovely thing she wants to do.

But as she stands there, she begins to weep. That is a womanly thing to do, isn't it? She weeps. We need to pay attention to these details. The harlot is no sob sister, for a woman who has been beaten and battered by life develops a hard shell. There comes a day when she is even harder than any man who comes along. But this one weeps. Our Lord has restored to her the badge of her womanhood, tears. This woman, had you met her before our Lord met her, would not have shed a tear. Now she weeps, and as she weeps the tears fall on the feet of Jesus. She's embarrassed when she sees what is happening. She looks for something to wipe them off, and there's nothing to use, so she lets down the tresses of her hair. With disheveled hair she weeps and wipes His feet, and as she wipes His feet she kisses them. It was the custom in that day to kiss the feet of a rabbi, and Luke's word is interesting: She "smothers" His feet with her kisses. Isn't that a lovely scene?

While this is going on our Lord seems to be ignoring the woman. He just continues to eat. And while He's eating, across the table from Him hard, critical, gimlet eyes are penetrating that scene. And if you think they are sympathetic, you are wrong.

Now when the Pharisee who had invited Him saw this, he spoke to himself. . . . (Luke 7:39)

He said nothing audibly—he's a suave, dapper man. He reveals nothing on the outside, but he's saying something to himself, not knowing the One sitting across from him is reading him like a book and that he might as well shout it from the housetop. Our Lord knew what he was thinking:

"This man, if He were a prophet, would know who and what manner of woman this is who is touching Him, for she is a sinner." (Luke 7:39)

What a scene this is. Our Lord is paying no attention

to the woman; the woman, disheveled hair, weeping and wiping His feet and kissing them; old Simon the Pharisee, hard-hearted, religious, criticizing, looking over and thinking, *Ah hah! He's no prophet. I knew all along He wasn't a prophet. If He were a prophet He would not permit a woman like that to touch Him.*

Notice what happens. This man Simon thought he saw it all and that Jesus was seeing nothing.

> **And Jesus answered and said to him, "Simon, I have something to say to you." So he said, "Teacher, say it."** (Luke 7:40)

In other words, our Lord said, "Simon, I have an after-dinner story to tell you." And Simon said, "This has certainly been an interesting meal, but You go ahead and tell Your story." Now our Lord uses sparkling and scintillating satire to make a point. He uses the rapier of sarcasm, not to wound or hurt this man, but as a scalpel to operate on the awful, festering sore that is in his soul. It's a simple story, actually not much to it, but oh, there's a point!

> **"There was a certain creditor who had two debtors. One owed five hundred denarii, and the other fifty. And when they had nothing with which to repay, he freely forgave them both. Tell Me, therefore, which of them will love him more?"** (Luke 7:41, 42)

A simple story, isn't it? Here is a man who has two debtors. Putting it in our legal tender, one of them owes him five hundred dollars, and the other man owes him fifty dollars. One man owes him ten times as much as the other. He calls them both in and he says to them, "You say you can't pay, you have nothing, so I cancel both debts. They have been paid as far as I'm concerned." Which will love him the most?

Our Lord is now trying to reach the heart of a Pharisee, and He is letting this man Simon judge himself. That is the way our Lord did these things. Oh, the marvel of our Lord and the way He dealt with men and women!

Now see this:

Simon answered and said, "I suppose the one whom he forgave more."

Oh, isn't he self-satisfied!

And He said to him, "You have rightly judged." (Luke 7:43)

And now our Lord does something for the first time—

Then He turned to the woman and said to Simon, "Do you see this woman?" (Luke 7:44)

He has paid no attention to the woman until this moment. Now He turns and looks back at the woman at the same time He's talking to Simon. He says, "Simon, do you see this woman? You thought you saw her and that I didn't see her. Well, you didn't see her, but I did see her! What do you see, Simon? Do you see a sinful woman? I see a sinful woman, but I see a forgiven sinner, and you don't see that. You see what she was. I see what she is."

It is interesting that the world will always judge you by the last sin you committed—"Simon, I see this woman. You don't see this woman."

Then He moves on and, my friend, our Lord does a very daring thing—a bold thing. Notice this very carefully.

> **"I entered your house; you gave Me no water for My feet, but she has washed My feet with her tears and wiped them with the hair of her head."** (Luke 7:44)

Our Lord counted every tear she shed. He knew every bit of it.

> **"You gave Me no kiss, but this woman has not ceased to kiss My feet since the time I came in. You did not anoint My head with oil, but this woman has anointed My feet with fragrant oil."** (Luke 7:45, 46)

Our Lord now contrasts these two. Notice that He does not contrast them on a theological level. I am sure that the woman did not know as much about the Book of Daniel as the Pharisee did. I'm confident of that. I'm confident that if you wanted a teacher for a Bible class, you never would have called on this woman. You might have asked the Pharisee. I'm

sure you would have because he knew the Law. Our
Lord did not even contrast them on the moral level
because one is the antithesis of the other, and what
a sharp contrast is here. He is a Pharisee; she is a
prostitute, or she was. He is the acme of morality;
she had sunk to the depths of immorality. He is the
product of religion; she is the product of the underworld. He sits there in self-satisfaction, and she
stands there embarrassed. Simon is offended by her
and shocked by her presence, but he needn't worry.
If you'd gone back just a few days, she would have
been brazen before him and would have had contempt for him and his kind. He is critical; she is
crying. He feels superior; she feels inferior. He is
from the upper stratum; she is from the lower
stratum. He represents the best; she represents the
worst. He is famous; she is notorious. He is from the
best section of town, from suburbia; she is from the
slums. He is a man of the boulevards; she is a woman
of the streets. He is a theologian; she is a tart. On a
moral level he is better than she. Our Lord didn't
make the contrast there.

My friend, will you notice now where our Lord
made the contrast. He stepped down into the life
where you and I walk in shoe leather, when you and
I show every minute of the day the kind of persons
we are. On the level of common courtesies, He said,
"Simon, when I came into your home after you
invited Me, you deliberately omitted the common
courtesy of putting out water for My feet, while this
woman has wet My feet with her tears. Simon, you
forgot to put oil on My head, and she has used

precious ointment on My feet. Simon, you ignored Me when I entered—you didn't even welcome Me with the kiss of greeting, and this woman has smothered My feet with kisses."

"Therefore I say to you, her sins, which are many, are forgiven, for she loved much. But to whom little is forgiven, the same loves little." (Luke 7:47)

Can you stand the exposure of this white light of heaven today? Christ put this moral Pharisee down by the side of a redeemed harlot, and under the scorching white light of heaven this Pharisee must have squirmed like a worm in hot ashes. He said to this Pharisee, "She is better than you are," and that burns in this day of hypocrisy, in this day when religion is a front, in this day when people are putting on airs. This will burn your soul, my friend, and you don't want to get too close to it.

Now He deals with her again personally, to give her assurance. She needs it.

Then He said to her, "Your sins are forgiven." (Luke 7:48)

He could have added, "Your sins have already been forgiven. I'm on the way to the Cross now to die for the sins of the world." He's saying also, "Simon, she's the sinner, and she knows it. She has been forgiven, and she's grateful. You don't recognize that you are a sinner, but you are. You think that somehow or other you are good enough, that you can get by." Every person, including the harlot and the religious Pharisee, needs to be forgiven. And, my friend, you and I have to come to the same Cross.

I used to think that the grace of God was like pipes on an organ. If a fellow is a big sinner and he's way low down, God will go way down and get him. But if he's an upstanding person, the grace of God doesn't have to go down so far to get that one. My friend, the grace of God has to go down just as far to get you as it does to get the lowest sinner in the United States. It required the *death* of the Son of God to save us! And the death of Christ will save the worst sinner.

In my first pastorate in Nashville, Tennessee, after I was ordained, I followed one of the most godly men I have ever met, Dr. A. S. Allen. He was my encouragement and a man of great blessing to my heart. He told me many things when I came to the church. I was green. It was a city church, and I was a country preacher. One day he said, "You'll notice this couple, Mr. and Mrs. So-and-So. I'll tell you about them," and he did. Dr. Allen had enjoyed a ministry in Nashville that very few men have had anywhere. He was the preacher who included a ministry to the underworld. They had confidence in him. One day a girl in one of those houses of prostitution died, and he was asked to come in and have a service for her. That funeral was conducted inside the house, and gathered there were all the pimps and prostitutes. And Dr. Allen preached the gospel to them. The madam of that house received Christ.

She witnessed to all those girls before they left, then closed up the place and moved out. She married a retired policeman, and that's the couple Dr. Allen was telling me about.

They were in their sixties when I went there. You could tell she had been a beauty. She was one of the most cultured, refined persons I've ever met. The man she married was just about as crude as any I've known, but she had met him back in those early days.

Dr. Allen told me that when she joined the church, the women of the church would not accept her. So she quietly withdrew from the membership, but she and her husband would always come in and sit in the back.

When I called on them, she said to me, "Brother McGee, you may wonder why I'm not a member of the church." I said, "Yes, Dr. Allen has already told me." She said, "I don't want to push myself on anyone. I just want to come and sit in the back and hear the gospel." Then tears came down a face that one time was hardened, and she said, "Christ did so much for me when He saved me!" And she couldn't say any more, for she was sobbing.

I preached in that church for several years. As I looked over that congregation, I'd see lovely Southern ladies sitting there, including my mother, also my aunt, but that couple sat in the back. I want to say to you, there was nobody sitting there who was superior to that woman. She had been forgiven much, and I'm afraid there were some others in that congregation who had never shed a tear about their sins.

My friend, do your sins disturb you today? Or are you continuing in them and keeping up a front? Put yourself down beside the harlot who came into the Pharisee's house. It makes a scorching burn, does it not? Our Lord now turns to her and says, "Your faith has saved you"—she had no works—"go in peace." My friend, if you've never yet turned to the Lord Jesus, He is the only Savior, and whether you are a Pharisee or whether you are a sinner today, a great sinner like this woman, He can and will and wants to save you. But you'll have to trust Him. He said to her, "Your faith has saved you." Oh, I can't help believing that Simon the Pharisee got the point, saw himself in the white light of heaven, and turned to Christ.

CHAPTER 8

AN OLD PORTRAIT OF CHRIST
(LEVITICUS 1:1–10)

T hree short blocks from Dallas Seminary in Dallas, Texas, is Baylor Hospital. It was in that hospital back in 1961 that Mr. Sam Rayburn, Speaker of the House of Representatives of the United States, lay dying of cancer. The wife of one of these seminary boys was a nurse in that hospital. Both this seminary student and his wife became close friends of the chaplain there, a man who was a faithful witness for the Lord Jesus Christ in that place of sickness and death. He visited Speaker Sam Rayburn each day. When he first presented the claims of Jesus Christ to him, Mr. Rayburn responded, "I believe in God. But I don't know anything about this man Jesus that you are talking about."

I estimate that Mr. Rayburn had known at least eight presidents of the United States. In the course of his public life he met most of the great men of the world. President Kennedy made a long trip to spend a few moments with Sam Rayburn. But President

Kennedy couldn't have helped him then, even if he had spent millions. The outstanding cancer specialists from all over America were brought to Dallas. They prolonged his life, but they could not cure him. For this man there was no word of hope from the great ones of the earth. The only One who could have helped him is the One of whom he said, "I don't know anything about this man Jesus that you're talking about."

In this brief series on the person and work of Christ, I trust that we might introduce Him to someone who does not know Him any more than Mr. Rayburn did. Paul the apostle wrote at the end of his life when he was in prison: "That I may know Him and the power of His resurrection." Paul was not saying here that he did not know Jesus as Savior—he did. In fact, he probably knew Him better than anyone else. But having known our Lord as well as he did, Paul still wanted to know Him better. If you know Christ as Savior, we trust this series will also help you to know Him better and appreciate Him more.

We are addressing here two extreme groups: one group knows nothing about this Man Jesus, and the other group knows Him but shares the longing expressed by Paul, "That I may know Him and the power of His resurrection."

The Picture Album

Are you aware that God gave us pictures of Christ before He sent Him to earth? This was done so that folk would recognize Him and know who He was when He came. One of the ways of looking at the Old Testament is to think of it as an album, a picture album in which you have more pictures of Christ than of anyone else. In fact, while I may not always recognize Him, I do believe with all my heart that on every page of the Old Testament there is a picture of Christ, if only we had eyes to see Him. So let's turn back now to that old album and look together at an old portrait of Christ.

The pictures of Him that we will look at are found in the Book of Leviticus, one of the most important books, and some expositors consider it the greatest book, in the Bible. God opens it by giving five offerings or sacrifices to the nation Israel. I don't think that any of these were new. Probably they all had been in use before, but He gives them to the nation Israel now with the specific law for each of these offerings.

The five offerings all speak of Christ. Each one is a picture of Him. Each speaks of one facet of the Lord Jesus Christ's manifold and many-sided person.

The first three offerings are called sweet savor offerings: the *burnt offering*, the *grain offering*, and the *peace offering*. These three offerings are called sweet savor offerings because they set before us the person of Christ—as our substitute, in His loveliness, and as our peace (Leviticus 1–3).

The last two offerings, the *sin offering* and the *trespass offering*, are called non-sweet savor offerings. Actually, they are bitter because they speak of the work of Christ for us upon the Cross.

Now the offering that God put first and foremost is the burnt offering. God gave it first because to Him it comes first in importance. God is giving it from His viewpoint. Actually the burnt offering was the oldest offering known to man. It was the offering that Abel, the son of Adam, brought at the very beginning of the human family. And that's been the way to God from that day down to the present, if you please. Also you will find that Noah brought a burnt offering, Abraham brought a burnt offering, Isaac brought a burnt offering, and Jacob brought a burnt offering to God. It's the oldest offering, and it's the reason today that, when we do a study of paganism and heathenism, we find tribes that have a sacrifice somewhere in their religious rites which they had taken with them when they left the Tower of Babel and moved out into the darkness of the jungle and away from God. They took a sacrifice with them because God had made it very important at the beginning.

This sacrifice was all-important to God, so much so that when He gave the observance of the burnt offering to the nation Israel and gave them an altar for sacrifice, He actually called that altar by the name of the sacrifice. It is the "burnt altar," or we sometimes call it the brazen altar. But it's a burnt altar because the burnt sacrifice was the most important sacrifice that was placed on that altar.

A Picture of Christ

Now, friend, I want to let the Holy Spirit, if He will, apply some of the brushstrokes to this picture. He promised to do it. The Lord Jesus said, "I'm going to send the Holy Spirit, and when He comes He will take the things of Mine and show them unto you" (see John 16:14). So we trust that the Holy Spirit will make meaningful these brushstrokes and that before we are through you will see a wonderful picture of the Lord Jesus Christ.

Brushstroke 1—All on the Altar

Let's put down our first brushstroke here, the brushstroke that the Holy Spirit puts down.

> **"If his offering is a burnt sacrifice of the herd, let him offer a male without blemish; he shall offer it of his own free will at the door of the tabernacle of meeting before the LORD."** (Leviticus 1:3)

Now this is the burnt sacrifice. The word in the Hebrew is *olah*, and it means "that which ascends." It's a burnt sacrifice because it was consumed in its totality. All of it was put on the altar, all of it was consumed by fire, and the sweet savor ascended to God—nothing was left but ashes.

First of all let me say that the burnt sacrifice is what God the Father sees in Christ, not what you see. He sees a beauty in Him that you and I have never seen. He sees in Him a wonder and a glory that we cannot comprehend. When God speaks of

Him it is always in superlative terms: "He is altogether *lovely*." "He's the *chiefest* of ten thousand." "This is My *beloved* Son, in whom I am *well-pleased*." What God the Father sees in Christ is the first brush stroke. Oh, my friend, our perception is so limited. It's not what you see in Him, but it's what the Father sees in the Son that is important. It's all-important.

Maybe at this time you are not satisfied in Christ. I have news for you: God is—God is satisfied with Him. Maybe you think that you ought to do something to gain your salvation. God says in effect, "I'm satisfied with what Jesus did for you on the Cross, and I'm not satisfied with you. Come to *Me*, presenting *His* sacrifice." It was a sweet-smelling savor to the Lord. Do you think God enjoyed smelling burnt meat? Then you don't know God. God didn't care for their offering when their hearts were not in it. He essentially says, "Away with your sacrifices. You missed the meaning of them. That burnt sacrifice should tell you what Christ means to Me. It should tell you how wonderful He is. It should tell you that Jesus is Mine, My Anointed One, My dearly beloved Son." Friend, that is what the sacrifice of Christ should tell us.

He doesn't want us to forget it. So He gives us a further symbolism. First the animal's inwards and legs are to be washed with water.

"And the priest shall burn all on the altar as a burnt sacrifice, an offering made by fire, a sweet aroma to the LORD." (Leviticus 1:9)

Burn *all* on the altar; all was to be consumed. This is what the apostle Paul meant when he wrote:

And walk in love, as Christ also has loved us and given Himself for us, an offering and a sacrifice to God for a sweet-smelling aroma. (Ephesians 5:2)

In other words, "Maybe you don't like it that Christ died on the Cross, but God does. Maybe you aren't concerned, but God is. Maybe you are not involved. God is! It is all-important to Him!"

Brushstroke 2—That Which Is Dear

Now notice another brushstroke:

"Speak to the children of Israel, and say to them: 'When any one of you brings an offering to the LORD, you shall bring your offering of the livestock—of the herd and of the flock.'" (Leviticus 1:2)

That further accentuates the value God places on the offering of Christ. Did you notice that carnivora are excluded? Wild animals were never accepted as a burnt offering. It was always domesticated animals that were used—animals that were tame, animals that were closer to man, those animals that had become pets, that would obey you and had become dear to you. And, of course, they were to be in the classification of clean animals. Those are the ones that represented Christ. How dear He was to God the Father!

I went hunting up in the Tehachapi Mountains many years ago. Friends of ours had a ranch up there. Oh, they had a wonderful spread for dinner— we had been out hunting all morning and were hungry! After dinner they started doing something that I didn't like. They began to kill some lambs they had on their ranch. They explained that because of the fact that ewes can't take care of twins up there, every time twins were born, both would die. So in order to make sure that one lived, they killed the other one. They were killing those off, just butchering them. I said, "Do you mind giving me one?" Of course they were more than willing, so we found a box and I brought a little lamb back to Pasadena.

I kept it until the little fellow grew up and started annoying the neighbors. Early in the morning he was ready to eat, and he was letting us know he was ready to eat. We even fed him with a bottle, and it's amazing how you can get attached to an animal like that.

Then there came that day when we had to get rid of that lamb, and I decided to butcher it. I had worked one time in a slaughterhouse, so I was going to butcher it myself. My wife took our daughter and went off for the day. She said, "I can't stand to see it. And I don't see how you can be that brutal!" Well, I got the little fellow—he would come right to me to be petted. So I strung him up on an apricot tree, head down. Then I sat down, and for about thirty minutes I just looked at him, afraid to touch him. Finally I had to screw up my courage, so I went on up to him, shut my eyes, and I slaughtered him. I felt bad for six months after that. I felt like I had done the meanest, the worst thing anyone can do—killing that innocent little lamb.

And I'll tell you what else I thought of. I thought of the Lamb of God who takes away the sin of the world. Have you ever stopped to think what Jesus meant to His Father? Have you ever considered what it meant in heaven when He suffered and died down here? Do you think heaven was unconcerned? It seems that God directed His people, "You take for a burnt offering that domestic animal, one you're close to, one that's dear to you, and you'll understand a little better how I feel, because Jesus is dear to Me." God spared not His own Son, but delivered Him up for us all. That, my friend, was a tremendous sacrifice!

Brushstroke 3—Without Blemish

Let me put on another brushstroke.

"If his offering is a burnt sacrifice of the herd, let him offer a male without blemish." (Leviticus 1:3)

A male without blemish. Male speaks of strength. It speaks of the ability of the Lord Jesus Christ to save. "Mighty to save" is the expression the Word of God uses. Another is "He is able to save to the uttermost." And then we are told, "He was without blemish," ideally perfect, "in Him was no sin." No sin was found in Him. Judas, after he had betrayed Him, confessed, "I have betrayed innocent blood."

Our Lord Jesus was a male without blemish. That's not all.

Brushstroke 4—Of His Own Free Will

"He shall offer it of his own free will at the door of the tabernacle of meeting before the LORD." (Leviticus 1:3)

His own free will. This is one sacrifice that God did not require. If any man offered this, it was his own voluntary will. And God emphasized this at the very beginning. "Speak to the children of Israel, and say to them: 'When any one of you'" . . . anyone, *any* one. He means you, but, my friend, you'll have to do it of your own free will. God this very day could force our nation to recognize His Son, but He won't. Each of us must come voluntarily to Christ.

He also said to them that "the door of the tabernacle" was the place where the burnt offering was to be presented to God. Why at the door of the tabernacle? Because if any man comes, he has to come God's way. The purpose was to keep Israel from idolatry since out yonder in the paganism and heathenism of that day, the burnt sacrifice was already being used in idolatry. God was emphatic: "My people are to bring it here to the door of the tabernacle. This is the only way." It has a message for us. Oh, will you look at this brushstroke for just a moment. It's to keep you and me from presuming we can come to God in our own way. We cannot. Jesus said, "No one comes to the Father except through Me" (John 14:6). You have to come by this brazen altar. You have to come bringing this sacrifice, which today is Christ. My friend, you and I cannot come to God any other way.

I have been greatly impressed, as I have ridden the freeways in Oklahoma City, Dallas, and Fort Worth, Texas, and here in Los Angeles, by the signs they have put up with these three words: Do Not Enter. I've never seen so many Do Not Enter signs. I got on the wrong road the other day after I was back in Los Angeles, and I found myself going to Bakersfield instead of returning home. I tried to get on the freeway. Mile after mile—Do Not Enter. I don't know who had been entering, but they certainly have adequate warning now. And I want you to know that I've learned enough about these freeways that when the sign says, Do Not Enter, I do not enter! You will be in trouble if you do.

Our Lord is also warning, "Do Not Enter," "Do Not Enter," on every one of the cults and isms in Southern California. In other words, He says to us, "You can't get to Me through this cult. You come to the door of the tabernacle, and I am the Door. By Me is the only way to God." That's dogmatic, and so is that sign, "Do Not Enter"—but you'd better obey it. And if you're going to get to God today, you come God's way. God says that Jesus Christ is the way that leads to Him. "I am the door. If anyone enters by Me, he will be saved, and will go in and out and find pasture" (John 10:9).

Brushstroke 5—A Substitute for Me

"Then he shall put his hand on the head of the burnt offering, and it will be accepted on his behalf to make atonement for him." (Leviticus 1:4)

It's a substitutionary sacrifice. That's what it taught. And laying the hand on the head of the little animal meant that it was designated and assigned for a particular purpose.

Remember when Paul and Barnabas went out as missionaries for the first time, the believers in Antioch laid their hands on them. Why? They were being set aside for a particular office. In the same way the laying on of hands in the levitical offering means first of all that the little animal is set aside for a definite purpose. It also has a spiritual message for us today, to convey and communicate invisible and intangible benefits. It meant to transfer sin. And every instructed and enlightened Israelite, when he put his hand on that little animal, understood that. He was confessing, "I deserve to die—the soul that sinneth, it shall die—but I have now put my hand on the little animal, and it takes my place, and what happens to this little animal should be happening to me." God told them, "For the life of the flesh is in the blood, and I have given it to you upon the altar to make atonement for your souls" (Leviticus 17:11).

As Hebrews 9:22 points out, "without shedding of blood there is no remission"—no forgiveness. It was to be an atonement, we are told here. The word *atonement* means "to cover up," and that's all it means. You won't find the word *atonement* in the New Testament. It's not there because now that Christ has come, God no longer covers up; rather, He *takes away* sins. They are blotted out. And may I say, the message here is that you and I come by faith. By faith we put our hand on Christ, and He becomes our substitute, dying in our stead. His death is acceptable to God. Nothing you and I do is acceptable to God. You and I need a substitute—Christ is that substitute.

Brushstroke 6—He Had to Die

Now will you notice:

"He shall kill the bull before the LORD; and the priests, Aaron's sons, shall bring the blood and sprinkle the blood all around on the altar that is by the door of the tabernacle of meeting." (Leviticus 1:5)

The animal had to die the minute it became a substitute. Our Lord died, the just for the unjust. He died, the innocent for the guilty. He died as the sinless One for those who are sinners. He died a substitutionary death for you and for me.

Sometimes the question is asked, "Who killed Christ?" And, as you know, around Eastertime that is batted back and forth. They blame Israel for it. But not only Israel; they blame the Roman government. May I say something that I trust will not offend you, but *you* killed Christ. I killed Him. If I had not been a sinner, He would not have died. His dying is a substitutionary death. God would not have let Him die unless He was bearing our sin, dying in our stead.

Brushstroke 7—What God Sees in Christ

But there is something else—first the priest was to wash the animal's inwards and legs with water:

"And the priest shall burn all on the altar as a burnt sacrifice, an offering made by fire, a sweet aroma to the LORD." (Leviticus 1:9)

Actually, not only was all of it consumed, but if we read further we would find that the ashes of both the wood and the sacrifice were gathered up and taken outside the camp. Now what is the significance of this? May I say to you, this is what God sees in Christ.

As you well know, God has been dishonored down here in this world. Men, women, and even children are dishonoring Him today. Remember King Belshazzar when he did that blatant and blasphemous thing of bringing the holy vessels from the temple into his banquet and using them in his drunken orgy. Then Daniel was brought in, and Daniel said to Belshazzar, "The God who holds your breath in His hand and owns all your ways, you have not glorified" (Daniel 5:23). Friend, that could be said of you, and that could be said of me. We do not glorify God. That's our problem.

We're great at glorifying ourselves, aren't we? We like to talk about what we have done when we ought to be talking about what He has done. We like to talk about who we are, but we ought to talk about who He is. May I say to you, God is not being glorified in the country in which we live. And we won't get by with it either. We are His creatures. He says that He must be glorified. The catechism asks the question, "What is the chief end of man?" and answers it, "The chief end of man is to glorify God and enjoy Him forever."

There had to be a man who glorified God fully and completely. And that man was Jesus Christ. In Psalm 40 we hear our Lord as He speaks from the Old Testament:

> **Many, O LORD my God, are Your wonderful works**
> **Which You have done;**
> **And Your thoughts toward us**
> **Cannot be recounted to You in order;**
> **If I would declare and speak of them,**
> **They are more than can be numbered.**
> **Sacrifice and offering You did not desire;**
> **My ears You have opened.**
> **Burnt offering and sin offering You did not require.**
> **Then I said, "Behold, I come;**
> **In the scroll of the book it is written of me.**
> **I delight to do Your will, O my God,**
> **And Your law is within my heart.**
> (Psalm 40:5–8)

Here is the Man who came into this world, who delighted to do the will of God, and who did it. No other man has done that. Adam failed; Abraham failed; Moses failed; David failed; Paul failed. And you have failed, and I have failed. But Jesus alone glorified God.

It is important to realize that the fire of the burnt sacrifice on the burnt altar does not speak of judgment. It speaks of the restless and resistless energy of God. You see, the burnt sacrifice is God's view of Christ. There is no mention of man's sin in this sacrifice. It is the highest view we have of Him anywhere.

This is really an old portrait of Christ, and it actually corresponds to the Gospel of John. For all of these levitical offerings, you find a counterpart in one of the Gospels. For the burnt altar you'll find a counterpart in the Gospel of John, and that's the reason the words of our Lord from the cross as He bore our sins, "My God, My God, why have You forsaken Me?" are not recorded in John's Gospel. Jesus Christ is God—how can you separate God from God? So John doesn't record that cry, because perfection is what God sees in Christ.

Now I want you to notice something that is quite wonderful. Over in the sixth chapter of Leviticus, verse 10, we have the law of this offering:

"And the priest shall put on his linen garment, and his linen trousers he shall put on his body, and take up the ashes of the burnt offering which the fire has consumed on the altar, and he shall put them beside the altar."

They were to take up all the ashes, you see, and if you read on, you will find it was all taken outside the camp.

May I say to you, this does not speak therefore of self-sacrifice; it speaks of self-consecration, self-dedication. And when it's all consumed, it reminds us of the words of our Lord on the cross: "It is finished!" No more fire to burn, it is all consumed. He gave it all that you and I might be saved.

Don't you dare say that salvation is cheap. *You* can't pay anything for it because you haven't anything to pay. The richest man in America today can't buy it. But he can have it for nothing, and you can have it for nothing because God paid everything for it.

Brushstroke 8—Communion with God

Notice something else. This sacrifice is a communion. Oh, follow me carefully now. If you missed everything else, don't miss this. This is what God sees in Christ. And for you and me it's a communion.

What is communion with God? I'll tell you what I thought for years. I'm afraid I was like folk who go to church and want to be separated Christians and say, "I want to come to the communion table with reverence, and I want to think some very high, noble, fine thoughts."

What conceit! What arrogance to think that we can think something that's pleasing to God! For God says, "My thoughts are not your thoughts, nor are your ways My ways" (Isaiah 55:8). Have you ever tried to do some nice thinking? I tried this while traveling on the train one time. I had quite a few hours to think. I don't know about you, but I can think of the dirtiest things when I'm trying to think nice thoughts! And that's what you do too, because you have the same kind of nature I have, and so do all these pious folk today who say, "We're going to think some nice thoughts." Oh, my friend, that's not having communion with Him. Do you know what communion is? This burnt offering tells us. It's when you and I think what God the Father thinks about Christ. That's communion. When you and I find in Christ our delight, when He becomes as wonderful to us as He is to God, then you are having communion, beloved, and not until then. You have to think God's thoughts after Him. My friend, to have communion with God it must be centered about the One He loves supremely, His beloved Son. The minute you become occupied with Christ, you are having communion with God. For the Old Testament Israelite, this voluntary burnt offering that prefigured Christ was a communion with God.

Brushstroke 9—Covered by His Righteousness

May I add one final touch? In Leviticus 7:8, we have more concerning the law of this offering. A while ago I said all of the animal was consumed, but I had not told the entire story. Notice this:

"And the priest who offers anyone's burnt offering, that priest shall have for himself the

skin of the burnt offering which he has offered."

The priest could take no part of the burnt offering as he did of the other offerings. With the other offerings he was given the choice cuts of the meat, but not out of this one. The one exception to the fact that all was to be consumed is that the skin or hide of the animal was to be given to the priest.

The portrait of Christ would not be complete without mentioning the robe of righteousness which Christ's death has provided for us. So when that man brought his sacrifice and offered that little lamb, he took a knife and slit its throat. The priests were then to take this offering, skin it, and burn every part of it on the altar except that skin. The priest was to have it. It pictures the garment that covers us as believers—that is, the *righteousness* of Christ, the robe of His righteousness. Although this offering does not speak of sin, it does demonstrate that there has to be a death. And our Lord Jesus Christ was obedient to death. He came as the Lamb of God who not only takes away our sin but also imputes to us His righteousness!

We read in Matthew 22 a parable our Lord told about a great wedding feast provided by a king for his son. Everybody was invited. The host sent servants out on the highways to invite folk to come in. But, my friend, if you're going to a wedding that is formal, you had better wear the right garment.

One man said, "It doesn't make any difference; I'll wear my sport shirt," and he went in.

The host came by and said, "Where's your wedding garment? I sent you one."

"Well, I didn't think it was important to wear it."

"I'll show you how important it is!" The rude guest was thrown out.

My friend, in other words God is saying today, "I've provided for you adequately. I gave My only begotten Son, in whom I delight. I didn't spare Him from paying the awful price for your sins, from dying for you. And today by faith in Him, His righteousness can cover you, so that you can be accepted in the Beloved. That's the only way you are acceptable to Me."

CHAPTER 9

WHY JESUS WAS ANGRY
(MARK 3:1–6)

It is assumed today that the gentle Jesus, the lowly carpenter of Nazareth, the humble peasant of Palestine, the man of Galilee, never exhibited any feelings of anger. Many are convinced that He evidenced no emotion of animosity, that He displayed no resistance to evil, and that He demonstrated no antagonism toward anything. The popular conception of Jesus is that He was the personification of pacifism, the ideal of nonresistance, the incarnation of the world's definition of meekness. Men today think of Him as the first-century Gandhi. They say He was neutral on every question and broadminded on every subject. The image of Jesus that liberalism has presented is absolutely foreign to the Word of God; and many Americans, after feeding on this pious pablum for several decades, think of a Jesus who never did exist.

The popular picture of Him is a monstrosity. Liberalism's Jesus was not actually a man. He had ice water for blood, a water pump for a heart, a gasoline motor for a nervous system, an IBM computer for a brain, and a tape recorder for a mouth. He was insensitive to evil, unmoved by sin. He was incapable of hating anything—anger was foreign to Him. *This* is not the Jesus recorded in Scripture.

Jesus Was Angry

A close and careful examination of the Gospels reveals our Lord as having an intense and passionate hatred of evil. He denounced sin and demonstrated against it courageously on every occasion. The fact of the matter is, if you read the Gospels from this viewpoint you might even go to the opposite extreme and present Him as the first "angry young man"!

At the beginning of His ministry He cleansed the temple. At the conclusion of His earthly ministry He cleansed the temple. Each time evildoers fled before Him. Why do you think they fled from Him?

During my first pastorate, in Nashville, Tennessee, I often played handball and tennis with a man who was a liberal preacher. He was a very fine man personally but a graduate of a liberal seminary in New York City. That was in the days of pacifism, and one day, after we had finished playing, he said, "I understand you preach that Jesus drove the money changers out of the temple and that He had a whip made of ropes that He would have used on those people. You don't really think that the gentle

Jesus would ever have used that whip of ropes, do you?"

I said to him, "I have only one question to ask you, and it is this: Was He bluffing?" You think that over for a while. Do you think Jesus was bluffing when He made that whip? May I say to you, when those money changers began to scatter to the four winds, they scattered because there was before them a Man big enough and angry enough to drive them out. He hated evil. This is the picture the Scripture presents of Him—not the willy-nilly, mollycoddled, shilly-shally Mr. Milquetoast type of Jesus that a great many would have us to believe He was.

Those money changers saw a man enraged and angry with sin. That hardened crowd—who knew they were breaking the Mosaic Law, who knew they were being irreverent, who knew they were defying God—do not think they would have fled had they not been afraid of the Man who was driving them out!

Then one day He stood and pronounced a woe upon the cities around the Sea of Galilee. "Woe to you, Chorazin! Woe to you, Bethsaida!" (Luke 10:13). He was deeply moved.

He stood over Jerusalem to pronounce judgment upon that city and said concerning it, "See! Your house is left to you desolate; for I say to you, you shall see Me no more till you say, 'Blessed is He who comes in the name of the LORD!'" (Matthew 23:38, 39). And as He said it, He *wept* over Jerusalem because He alone knew the judgment that was to fall upon the city in A.D. 70.

He pronounced woes against the scribes and Pharisees in the harshest denunciation that you will find in the Scripture (or out of the Scripture, for that matter), and it still scorches that page of the Word of God. Let us look at just one such statement as He was speaking to scribes and Pharisees: *"Serpents, brood of vipers! How can you escape the condemnation of hell?"* (Matthew 23:33, italics added). You cannot have language any stronger than that! And I cannot imagine the Jesus who used that language being unmoved when He spoke to the crowd there that day.

I want to lift out one isolated instance in His ministry in which He exhibited anger. Of all things, it was on the Sabbath day—a day on which most people not only put on a change of clothing but also put on a change of attitude as they come to church. They may not be sweet on other days, but they are generally sweet at church. However, our Lord wasn't sweet at church. He became angry. The record says that He was angry.

Will you listen to Mark as he records this incident?

And He entered the synagogue again, and a man was there who had a withered hand. So they watched Him closely, whether He would heal him on the Sabbath, so that they might accuse Him. (Mark 3:1, 2)

I cannot prove this, but I think these verses would indicate that the man was "planted" there by the

Pharisees and the scribes. He was placed there, but not because they wanted him healed; they didn't care what happened to that man. They were not even concerned about him. They placed him there because they wanted to trap the Lord Jesus. They were after Him.

Our Lord came and saw the situation.

And He said to the man who had the withered hand, "Step forward." (Mark 3:3)

Although the man with the withered hand had been placed there as a trap, that did not make any difference to our Lord. He was going to do something for him. But before He did:

Then He said to them, "Is it lawful on the Sabbath to do good or to do evil, to save life or to kill?" But they kept silent. (Mark 3:4)

Candidly, they did not care. They didn't care whether that man was healed or not. They were concerned about a religious ritual—that was all. They were as hard as anyone could possibly be; they had no concern whatever for that man. "They kept silent." They didn't dare open their mouths.

And when He had looked around at them with anger, being grieved by the hardness of their hearts, He said to the man, "Stretch out your hand." And he stretched it out, and his hand was restored as whole as the other. (Mark 3:5)

Jesus was angry. He was angry with the hard hearts of the religious rulers. That was the thing that made Him angry on the Sabbath day when He went into the synagogue.

May I say this: *If Jesus had not been angry, He would not have been God.*

God Was Angry

You may say, "Oh, you surely don't believe His anger proved that He was God!" I certainly do—because the God who is presented in the Word of God, whether you like it or not, is a God who exhibits wrath and anger against sin. He has always done so.

Back in the Old Testament again and again He exhibited anger against sin. There are over one hundred statements in the Old Testament that say that God was angry. Oh, I know that it is not popular today to say that God ever becomes angry, but God is angry with sin.

We have looked at one incident of anger in the life of our Lord. Now let us turn back to the Old Testament and pick out one isolated instance there.

From 1 Kings 11:9, I lift out this statement, "So the LORD became angry with Solomon." Why in the world was God angry with Solomon? Well, let's read the whole passage.

So the LORD became angry with Solomon, because his heart had turned from the LORD God of Israel, who had appeared to him twice.

Solomon had a unique privilege. This man dedicated the temple, and when he did so, the glory of the Lord filled that temple. Not many men ever had that privilege. But Solomon's heart was turned away from the Lord because he married many foreign women who worshiped false gods. There are people today who say, "Why did God permit Solomon to have so many wives?" God *didn't* permit it. God was angry with Solomon. Someone will say, "But God allowed it, didn't He?" Yes, because God will not interfere with your free will as a believer. If you go into sin, He will let you. He let Solomon because He will not interfere with a man's free will. But may I say again, *God was angry with Solomon* for allowing his idolatrous wives to turn him away from Him.

"Well, God didn't do anything about it."

Yes, He did. Just as the death of Christ rent in two the veil in the temple, so God reached to the top of the kingdom, and right down through that kingdom He made a rent—dividing the kingdom because of Solomon. *God was angry with Solomon.*

I challenge anyone to show me in the Word of God any instance in which God has ever compromised with evil or with sin. He hates it. He says He hates it. The record states that when Solomon, one of His own, went into sin, God was angry with him. God did not approve of what this man did. As far as I am concerned, I would not want to have been in Solomon's shoes.

God, in the Old Testament, was angry with sin; and when the Lord Jesus Christ, God incarnate, walked this earth in human flesh, *He* was angry with sin. On every occasion He revealed His antagonism toward it.

Christians Are to Be Angry

If you think the things we have been saying are strange, this may really startle you. *The Christian is commanded to be angry!*

Somebody will say, "Wait a minute now, preacher. You've gone too far! I happen to know that anger is a sin. The Bible says anger is a sin. Paul, in Ephesians 4:31, says, 'Let all bitterness, wrath, anger, clamor, and evil speaking be put away from you, with all malice.' And now you say that God commands us to be angry?"

Yes. God commands us to be angry.

Now, there is an anger that is a sin. When it is this old flesh of ours that flares up because of some little slight to our ego, that is sin. But, my friend, anger is not always a sin for a believer, for he is commanded to be angry. Christ commands the believer to be angry.

Paul, writing to the Ephesians in this same chapter, says, "Be angry, and do not sin" (Ephesians 4:26). The believer is commanded to be angry. Will you notice this very carefully: Christian character is evidenced by that which makes one angry.

This tremendous thing was said of Gaston de Foix: "He loved what ought to be loved, and he hated what ought to be hated, and he was never destitute of conscience on anything." How wonderful to be that kind of man—to love what should be loved and to hate what should be hated and to have a conscience on everything.

The trouble with believers today is that we have taken so many spiritual tranquilizers that we exhibit no resentment against evil at all. We want to be broad-minded; and believe me, we are!

Dr. Thomas Arnold, the man who made Rugby one of the greatest schools the world has ever seen, said this: "I was never sure of a boy who only loved the good. I was not sure of him until he began to hate the evil."

There are a lot of folk today who are syrupy. They exhibit and exude saccharine sweetness. They just *love* the good, but it is another thing to hate the evil. What is *your* attitude, really?

"To be incapable of moral indignation against wrong is to lack real love for the right," according to Dr. Augustus H. Strong. And Xenophon was intending to compliment his enemy, Cyrus the Younger, when he said concerning him that he did more good for his friends and more harm to his enemies than any man who had ever lived up to that time. Cyrus had feelings of right and wrong. He loved the good, but when he loved the good, he hated the evil.

Dr. William G. T. Shedd says, "Human character is worthless in proportion as abhorrence of sin is lacking in it."

Charles II was called the "merry monarch," and the record of his reign is a most sordid story. There came a day when the merriment ended and a terrified Charles faced death unprepared. But of his life it was said, "He felt no gratitude for benefits and no resentment for wrong. He did not love anyone and he did not hate anyone. He was indifferent to right and wrong, and the only feeling that he had for anyone and everyone was contempt."

I would hate to be that kind of person, wouldn't you? I would not care to be one who could move through life today and have no feeling about anything around me—not loving the good and not hating the evil. And yet there are many believers today who think it is Christian conduct to exhibit no feeling at all about anything.

Our Lord, when He moved through this earth, exhibited feeling that was intense—a passion against evil.

Paul wrote a letter to the Corinthians in which he rebuked them severely. "You are over there arguing about whether Paul or Apollos or Simon Peter is the greatest preacher, and many of you like to say, 'I follow this one,' or, 'I follow that one.' Baby talk! You are babies, carnal Christians, arguing about that sort of thing. You have no feeling about evil. It is in your midst, and you won't do a thing about it!" And Paul called it by name. He marked it out, and then he said, "If you don't do something about it, I will when I come!"

The church in Corinth was stung to the very quick. It went to its knees in prayer, and its conscience became sharpened again. The Corinthians said to the man who had done wrong, "You are wrong." They were angry.

And then Paul wrote a second letter to them in which he said this:

For observe this very thing, that you sorrowed in a godly manner: What diligence it produced in you, what clearing of yourselves, what indignation, what fear, what vehement desire, what zeal, what vindication! In all things you proved yourselves to be clear in this matter. (2 Corinthians 7:11)

Paul says, "What indignation!" He loved it!

William Lecky, in his book *Democracy and Liberty*, said this: "There is one thing worse than corruption, and that is acquiescence in corruption."

Herbert Spencer said that "good nature, with Americans, has become a crime and that because of our good nature, we feel as much goodwill for evil as for good." How accurate he was!

What Angers You?

What makes you angry today? If it is some little personal resentment or some little personal slight, then it is sin. But can you shut your eyes to evil? Can you see that which is wrong, even in your church, and say nothing? Can you? Can you open your ears to gossip and listen to it and then walk away unmoved and do nothing about it? God have mercy on you if you can! That is not Christian.

"What indignation!" Paul said, "I want to congratulate you, that you didn't shut your eyes to evil in the church." Does the indifference, the coldness, and the apostasy of this hour leave you unmoved? Are you, in the midst of an apostate church, like a limp dishrag, flopping back and forth, agreeing with every crowd and going with every group? May I say to you, we need spiritual backbone that will stand up and say to a man, "You are wrong, and I am opposed to what is wrong."

A certain monk took pleasure in antagonizing Martin Luther. The great reformer whipped him down intellectually, for Luther was a brilliant man. But the monk in a very stubborn way kept baiting him. Luther once said to him, "I will break in pieces your heart of brass and pulverize your iron brains." Martin Luther said that! Do you know why? Because the man would not see the gospel of the grace of God, that men are justified by faith. It made Martin Luther angry.

The Wrath of the Lamb

Let us come back now to the Lord Jesus. We looked at incidents in His earthly ministry. We went back to the Old Testament and saw that God was angry in the past. I want us to move into the future now and take one final look at Him. Will you listen to this language?

And the kings of the earth, the great men, the rich men, the commanders, the mighty men, every slave and every free man, hid them- selves in the caves and in the rocks of the

mountains, and said to the mountains and
rocks, "Fall on us and hide us from the face
of Him who sits on the throne and from the
wrath of the Lamb! For the great day of His
wrath has come, and who is able to stand?"
(Revelation 6:15–17)

"Do you mean to tell me a little *lamb* is angry?"
Yes.
"Do you mean to tell me men are going to run and
hide from a lamb?"
Yes.
"Well, they surely must be cowards to run from a
little lamb! Whoever heard of a little lamb hurting
anybody? Such a gentle little thing!"
The greatest deception the world will have, until
the Antichrist gets here, is the fabrication concern-
ing Jesus Christ—that He would not swat a fly, that
He would not crush a grape, that He is sort of a
first-century Mr. Milquetoast.
"Wasn't He a lamb?"
Yes. John marked Him out as a lamb.
"He was a lamb in His character?"
Yes. Meekness, humility, and gentleness characterized Him, but not the kind of meekness you have
in mind. It was not weakness—it was strength.
If you will read the Gospels very carefully, you
will find that only twice in His adult lifetime did He
ever obey any man or follow any human suggestion.
Did you ever notice that? He positively did not go
along with the crowd. His disciples said, "Send the
multitude away, that they may go into the village

and buy bread." Our Lord said, "You feed them." (See Luke 9:12, 13.) He is following nobody's suggestion.

A man came and said, "My little girl—she's dying! Oh, if You'll just come and heal her." Our Lord said, "Not now. There is a sick woman here. I want to heal her first, and it will be a little while before I get to your house." The servants came and said to the anxious father, "Your little girl is dead. You can leave Jesus alone now." Our Lord said, "I am coming, but not to heal the sick, as you thought I would. I am coming to raise the dead." He just simply did not follow men's directions.

Simon Peter said, "Don't go to Jerusalem and die on the cross!" Our Lord said, "I am going to Jerusalem to die on the cross, regardless of what you say."

They said to Him, when He was hanging on the cross, "Come down from the cross." Of course He would not, because He was paying the penalty for the sins of the world.

When He was a boy of twelve, it is said:

Then He went down with them and came to Nazareth, and was subject to them, but His mother kept all these things in her heart. (Luke 2:51)

As an adult He was obedient to His Heavenly Father but did not take orders from man, until they came and arrested Him. From that moment on, He was the Lamb led to the slaughter, and He became "obedient to the point of death, even the death of the cross" (Philippians 2:8). The reason He hung there obediently, yielding Himself to the hatred of men, was because He was dying for your sin and mine. That was the only reason He was being obedient.

He is "the Lamb of God who takes away the sin of the world!" (John 1:29). And because He died for the sin of the world, a great many people say, "Well—a little lamb—I'm not afraid of Him!" My friend, you do well to be afraid of Him. And every believer does well to fear the Lord Jesus.

"Oh, don't say that! He is so gentle and so loving—I can go to Him." Yes, you can! But, my beloved, *He hates your sin.* He hates it! He is angry with your sin.

> **For we know Him who said, "Vengeance is Mine, I will repay," says the Lord. And again, "The LORD will judge His people." It is a fearful thing to fall into the hands of the living God.** (Hebrews 10:30, 31)

The writer to the Hebrews says, "It is a fearful thing to fall into the hands of the living God." Whom do you think he is talking about—the unsaved? No. "The Lord shall judge *His own people.*" The greatest deception held by Christians today is that they can go on being indifferent, living in sin, and saying, "I am going to get by with it." This is the reason we have so many psychosomatic disorders among believers. They are trying to "get by with it."

The further I go in my ministry and the more I

watch God's people, the more convinced I am that He is moving today. He is reaching in here and reaching in there, judging His own when they will not deal with the sin in their lives. My friend, we *must* recognize that "it is a *fearful* thing to fall into the hands of the living God!" He disciplines His own. Oh, He redeemed you, He died for you, and He loves you. But He hates your sin.

If God were to compromise with sin in my life, I should lose my respect for Him. But I have not lost and never will lose my respect for Him because I have learned that when McGee tries to explain it away, to excuse his sin somehow, *God does not.* "It is a fearful thing to fall into the hands of the living God."

If for the believer it is a fearful thing to fall into the hands of the living God, what about the unsaved? God hates sin; the Lord Jesus is angry with sin. And there is only one place to hide from the wrath of God, the wrath of the Lamb—only one place to hide.

After World War II a book came out bearing the title *No Place to Hide*, with the alarming message that there is no place to hide from an atomic bomb. It is a frightful and awful thing to find that we live in a world where there actually is no place to hide, no refuge to which one can flee.

But for the sinner there *is* a place to hide, and that is in the cleft of the Rock—that Rock, Christ Jesus, who was rent for us. There the storm of the wrath of God will pass over. But that is the only place. Do not deceive yourself with the idea that, because He is characterized as a lamb, He is not going to punish sin. He *is* going to punish sin. He *does* punish sin. The wrath of the Lamb is a reality.

However, that same Lamb was offered as a sacrifice on the Cross for you and for me. He took in His body, there on the Cross, all the wrath and judgment of a holy God against sin in order that you and I might be saved. He is the only place of safety today, and He invites you to accept the merit of His sacrifice and be safe. To accept His invitation is to find the one hiding place for a sin-troubled heart. To reject Him is to choose the wrath of the Lamb.

CHAPTER 10

WHO AM I?
(MATTHEW 16:13–19)

There has been more confusion concerning the person of Jesus Christ than of anyone else who has ever lived. There have been more differences of opinion regarding Him, and there have been more divisions made regarding His person than of anyone else. It has always been so.

Confusion among Men
Concerning the Person of Christ

When Jesus came into the region of Caesarea Philippi, He asked His disciples, saying, "Who do men say that I, the Son of Man, am?" So they said, "Some say John the Baptist, some Elijah, and others Jeremiah or one of the prophets." (Matthew 16:13, 14)

For two and a half years of our Lord's ministry, He walked in and out among folk. He taught as no other man had ever taught. He performed miracles; He expressed to men and women the longing of the

Father's heart for lost sinners. He mingled with the human family, speaking with individuals, rebuking religious rulers, and giving words of comfort to sinners. After these two and a half years, there was great confusion concerning His person, who He was. So He took His disciples aside to Caesarea Philippi, which was actually gentile territory, beyond the northern border of Judea, to a remote place away from the curious crowd and the caustic criticism of religious rulers.

Now when Jesus went into gentile territory, I think He had two purposes in mind. He went there for the sake of His disciples, that they might have clearly in their minds who He was. His second reason may have been the need to gird Himself for the task that was ahead of Him, because at Caesarea Philippi, six months before His crucifixion, He told these men for the first time that He was going to Jerusalem to die on the Cross. We can well understand that before this traumatic experience it was necessary for them to be clear as to who He actually was.

There are those today who are saying that it is not really important that we believe in the virgin birth of Christ or that we believe in His miracles or that we believe in His deity. After all, they say, you need only to believe in Jesus. That is the only thing that is essential. But may I say, you and I cannot trust Him unless we have confidence in His person. You and I cannot have a Savior unless He is every whit who He claimed to be. The real test for any of us is what we think of Christ.

"What think ye of Christ?" is the test,
    To try both your state and your scheme;
You cannot be right in the rest,
    Unless you think rightly of Him;
As Jesus appears in your view—
    As He is beloved or not,
So God is disposed to you,
    And mercy or wrath is your lot.

—John Newton

So when He took His disciples aside, He asked them this question first, "Who do men say that I, the Son of Man, am?" That is, "What is the thinking of folk yonder on the outside with whom I've come in contact? I've rubbed shoulders with them. I've spoken to them, and they've seen miracles performed. What do they think concerning Me? What is their estimate?"

Of course, the disciples had always mingled with the crowds also, and they had heard many things. So they gave Him a report, and you'll notice that all of them chimed in here, and I think each one of them mentioned something because He asked it of all of them. Maybe Thomas said, "Well, I've heard some of them say that You are John the Baptist," and I think probably John the apostle said, "I've heard some of them say that You are Elijah," and Andrew added, "But I've heard some of them say that You are Jeremiah." All of the disciples made a contribution. Then one of them, probably Philip since he was a very quiet fellow, spoke: "Or they say that You are one of the prophets." So you can see that there was a difference of opinion concerning who He was.

I suppose the majority of the people thought He was John the Baptist (John the baptizer). Many had heard this forerunner of Jesus speak, and probably most knew of his untimely decease. They knew how brutally and cruelly he had been beheaded and how this man's voice had been silenced because he stood out against evil in his day. He had actually had the courage to rebuke a king, and for that he was beheaded! And so there were those who believed that Jesus was John returned to life. To believe that, in my opinion, was superstition; but they believed it because the Lord Jesus had at the beginning picked up the same message that John the Baptist used: "Repent, for the kingdom of heaven is at hand." Also there was something about our Lord that reminded those who heard Him of John, so that some of them were saying, "I think He is John the Baptist." That was a great compliment, because even John's enemies regarded him as a prophet from God.

Then there were others who thought Jesus was Elijah, and there was scriptural basis for this. Elijah is the prophet they remembered above all the other prophets. He was probably the most courageous man who ever walked this earth. And, my friend, he walked alone with God. He had no one with whom he could fellowship. "Oh," you say, "there were seven thousand up yonder who had not bowed to Baal." Elijah didn't know them. And neither would Elijah be found hiding in a cave up in the mountains with the one hundred mentioned in 1 Kings 18:13.

This man was out in the open, standing alone against great odds. He stood against the evil of his day—Ahab and Jezebel—and you just won't find any who are worse than those two. What Ahab didn't think of, Jezebel did. Actually she thought of twice as much evil as Ahab thought of. She was one of the most wicked people who ever walked across the pages of Scripture, but this man Elijah is the one who stood against her and against the prophets of Baal. He made a great impression on his people. And, as you may remember, he did not die but was carried to heaven in a chariot of fire.

In the Book of Isaiah, and then Malachi 4:5 specifically, God had predicted Elijah's return: "Behold, I will send you Elijah the prophet before the coming of the great and dreadful day of the LORD." So you see, they had Scripture to believe that Elijah would return, and when our Lord Jesus came, rebuking the religious rulers and standing against evil, they said, "He is Elijah who has now come." May I say to you, that was a compliment—I can't conceive of a greater compliment than that.

Then there were others who thought Jesus was Jeremiah. When I read this I must confess that I am puzzled how anyone could imagine Him to be Elijah and then someone else imagine He could be Jeremiah, because Jeremiah was the opposite of Elijah. For example, I cannot find Elijah shedding a tear. I see no sympathy in that man whatever. He was as cold-blooded as they come. I see no sign of even weakness until that day he crawled under a juniper tree and said, "I want to die." But I can explain his condition at that time. He was physically exhausted, so much so that what he needed was good food and rest. He wasn't well when he made a statement like that, and the Angel of the Lord—who I believe was the preincarnate Christ—nursed him back to health. Oh, how tender our Lord was with His overwrought prophet! Do you know what Elijah did after he had recovered? Back into the court of Ahab and Jezebel he went, back again to bring anathema down upon them. That's Elijah.

But Jeremiah was entirely different. Emotional—he couldn't give out God's message of doom to his people without weeping. He was the weeping prophet of the Old Testament.

You say, well, why did God choose him as a prophet? Because God had to have that kind of man to give such a message. It was the harshest message of all. He said to the people of Judah, "You are going into captivity." He said, "God will destroy the temple and the city of Jerusalem." My friend, God doesn't want a harsh man to give a message like that. God wants a man with a tender heart. And this man Jeremiah had a heart of compassion for his people. He had a heart almost like a woman's. The statement he made was:

Oh, that my head were waters,
And my eyes a fountain of tears,
That I might weep day and night
For the slain of the daughter of my people!
(Jeremiah 9:1)

Finally he went to the Lord and said in effect, "If You don't mind, I'll resign. This thing is too difficult. I can't go on giving a message like this—it's breaking my heart." God said, "All right. If you want to resign, Jeremiah, you may."

And he did resign, but he came back and said, "Lord, Your Word was in me like fire in my bones, and when I tried to keep quiet, I couldn't. If You don't mind, I'll go back." He is God's man, and when you see him weeping, you know exactly how God feels about sending His people into captivity.

Therefore, the Lord Jesus reminded people of Jeremiah, especially when He sat and wept over the city, saying:

"O Jerusalem, Jerusalem, the one who kills the prophets and stones those who are sent to her! How often I wanted to gather your children together, as a hen gathers her chicks under her wings, but you were not willing!" (Matthew 23:37)

Then He added, "See! Your house is left to you desolate." He knew that city was to be destroyed just as it had been destroyed in the days of Nebuchadnezzar. But this time it would be destroyed by Titus the Roman, with just as much brutality, cruelty, and bloodshed. Like Jeremiah, our Lord wept over the city. It was a heartbreak to Him.

So some of the people thought He was Jeremiah, and rightly so, because He did shed tears. But what a contrast there was between Jeremiah and Elijah, and what a difference of opinion as to who Jesus was!

Then others in the crowd thought Jesus was just one of the prophets. May I say to you, everything they said was complimentary, but it fell far short of the true identity of Christ.

Also in our day, friend, to miss the fact that the Lord Jesus Christ is God incarnate is one of the most tragic blunders one can make. These folk in that day were making this blunder. Here He was, rubbing shoulders with them, and they were missing who He was! And certainly there was a divergence of opinion among them.

Confession of Peter about the Person of Christ

He said to them, "But who do you say that I am?" Simon Peter answered and said, "You are the Christ, the Son of the living God." (Matthew 16:15, 16)

Now He turns from the crowd outside to His own disciples. You must remember that He has been with them for two and a half years. They have been together constantly, day and night. Everything Jesus did was under their scrutiny. He could say to them, "Which of you convinces Me of sin?" And even Judas, for three years, kept his eyes on Christ. Oh, what a critic he was! Possibly he was thinking, *Just wait until He stubs His toe. I'll get Him*. But our Lord never stubbed His toe, and when Judas finally betrayed Him, he had to honestly confess, "I have betrayed *innocent* blood."

So, speaking directly to these men who have been with Him for two and a half years, He asks, "But who do *you* say that I am?" Now all these men are able to answer through their spokesman, Simon Peter. Will you listen to them now: "Simon Peter answered and said, 'You are the Christ, the Son of the living God!'" Peter could have said nothing higher than that. He was saying, "You are the Christ," that is, "You are the Messiah, the Anointed One, the One predicted in the Old Testament."

The psalmist David had said in Psalm 2 that "the kings of the earth set themselves, and the rulers take counsel together, against the LORD and against His Anointed." His "Anointed" is Christ, if you please. He is the One who is God's partner, God's equal, the Christ. Now Peter says to Jesus, "You are the Christ, the Son of the living God."

Isaiah 9:6 speaks of Christ in His second coming. "For unto us a Child is born, unto us a Son is given." Notice that the Child was born; the Son was *given* (not born) because He is the eternal Son of God, and God the Father is the eternal Father. My friend, when you have an eternal Father, you have to have an eternal Son. And when you have both an eternal Father and an eternal Son, you never have any begetting. The Lord Jesus has always been God the Son. And when He was put on trial, these religious rulers who knew the Old Testament Scriptures pointedly asked Him, "Are You the Christ, the Son of the Blessed?" Remember what His answer was—

He was under oath at the time—He said, "I am. And you will see the Son of Man sitting at the right hand of the Power, and coming with the clouds of heaven" (Mark 14:62). He made the highest claim that anyone could possibly make for that title, "Son of Man." It is on an equal with the title "Son of God" or "Son of the Blessed."

Now may I say to you, Peter and the other disciples are accurate on the person of Christ when they say, "You are the Christ, the Son of the living God." They have been with Him for two and a half years— they know who He is.

Our Lord now speaks to them. Will you notice this very carefully:

Jesus answered and said to him, "Blessed are you, Simon Bar-Jonah, for flesh and blood has not revealed this to you, but My Father who is in heaven." (Matthew 16:17)

In other words, you cannot come to this estimate of the Lord Jesus Christ unless the Holy Spirit of God opens your eyes to Him. Paul says, "No one can say that Jesus is Lord except by the Holy Spirit" (1 Corinthians 12:3). Oh, I don't mean just to say the word *Lord,* because many use that word. But I am saying that no one can acknowledge Him as Lord in their heart unless the Holy Spirit reveals Him. And the Lord Jesus Himself said that when the Holy Spirit has come, "He will take of what is Mine and declare it to you" (John 16:14).

Friend, that is why the Bible is different from any

other book in existence today. Any book that any person ever wrote can be figured out by another person. I remember what my geometry teacher used to say when I'd come to school many a time frustrated and complaining, "Nobody can work this problem!" He would say, "There never could be a problem made by a person that another person couldn't work out." And, friend, you cannot find anything that anyone can write or do that cannot be figured out by someone else.

But here is a book that is different from any other. You will not, nor can you, understand it, nor will you ever know the person of Jesus Christ until the Holy Spirit opens your eyes to see Him in all His winsomeness, in all His loveliness, and in all the glory of His person. I am not disturbed today to hear an unbeliever say, "I do not believe in the deity of Christ." Actually, if he says he *does* believe in the deity of Christ, something is wrong. You can't believe in His deity until the Holy Spirit of God makes Him real to you. Our Lord said, "Simon Bar–Jonah . . . flesh and blood has not revealed this to you, but My Father who is in heaven."

Construction of the Church on the Person of Christ

Jesus answered and said to him, "Blessed are you, Simon Bar-Jonah, for flesh and blood has not revealed this to you, but My Father who is in heaven. And I also say to you that you are Peter, and on this rock I will build My

church, and the gates of Hades shall not prevail against it." (Matthew 16:17, 18)

I think these verses and the succeeding verse are probably more misunderstood in Christendom today than any other three verses. We miss in our English translation the play on words that is here. Our Lord used two Greek words for the English word *rock*. The Lord Jesus, speaking to Peter, said, "You are *Petros*, and on this *petra* I will build My church." In other words, "You are a little rock, you're just a pebble"—and that's all we are, just little pebbles on the beach—"but on the bedrock I will build My church."

This is the first time that Christ mentioned His church, and He mentioned it only twice. He said, "I *will* build. . . ." At that time the church was in the future. The church came into existence after His resurrection, on the Day of Pentecost.

What did He mean when He said to Peter, "I will build My church on the rock"? He certainly didn't mean He would build it on Simon Peter because He changed the word altogether. He didn't say, "You are *Petros*, and on this *Petros* I will build My church." He said, "You are a little rock, and I'll build My church on the foundation rock." What is that foundation? I hear people say, "It is your confession of faith in Christ." Absolutely not. What is the foundation on which the church is built? What is the rock on which the church is built? First Corinthians makes it abundantly clear: "For no other foundation can anyone lay than that which is laid, which is Jesus Christ" (1 Corinthians 3:11). Our Lord is the foundation on which the church is built.

Did Peter understand it this way? He most surely did. Speaking of Christ, he wrote:

Coming to Him as to a living stone, rejected indeed by men, but chosen by God and precious. (1 Peter 2:4)

I think it is so interesting how Simon Peter, that big, rugged fisherman, repeats the word *precious,* which we tend to think of as a woman's word. But Peter, speaking of Christ or of His blood or any part of Him, uses the word *precious.*

Peter says Christ is a living stone. But how are we living stones? We have been born again by the Word of God.

You also, as living stones, are being built up a spiritual house, a holy priesthood, to offer up spiritual sacrifices acceptable to God through Jesus Christ. Therefore it is also contained in the Scripture, "Behold, I lay in Zion/ A chief cornerstone, elect, precious,/ And he who believes on Him will by no means be put to shame." (1 Peter 2:5–6)

Simon Peter understood absolutely that not he but the Lord Jesus Christ is that cornerstone:

Therefore, to you who believe, He is precious [a better translation would be, "for you who believe is the preciousness"]**; but to those who are dis-**

obedient, "The stone which the builders re-
jected/ Has become the chief cornerstone." (1
Peter 2:7)

When He came into the world He was rejected by
His own people—"He came to His own, and His own
did not receive Him" (John 1:11). Not only then was
He rejected, but you and I live today in a Christ-re-
jecting world. Peter was saying, "The Lord Jesus
Christ is the stone. He is the Rock on which the
church is built." And, my friend, your confession,
my confession, and Simon Peter's confession establish us as little rocks on Christ the solid Rock. That
is the thing our Lord is saying to this man Peter.

Clarification on the Keys of the Kingdom

As Jesus continues to speak to Peter, He says
something else that is very significant to you and
me. It also has been greatly misunderstood:

**"And I will give you the keys of the kingdom
of heaven, and whatever you bind on earth
will be bound in heaven, and whatever you
loose on earth will be loosed in heaven."** (Matthew 16:19)

What did He mean by this? Did Christ mean that
He was actually giving to Simon Peter some keys,
and whatever Simon Peter would bind on earth
would be bound in heaven, or loosed on earth would
be loosed in heaven? Yes, He meant that. Were they

given only to Simon Peter? No, Jesus gives them to those who make the same confession made by Peter, those who know Christ as Savior. If you are a child of God, you have these keys as well as any other believer has them. The keys were the badge of authority for the office of the scribes who interpreted the Scriptures to the people, as in Nehemiah's day (see Nehemiah 8:1–8). When Nehemiah wrote, there probably were no more than two copies of the Scriptures in existence. Multitudes of the people who returned to the land of Israel after seventy years of captivity had never heard the Word of God. So the people were called together, and they had the greatest Bible reading on record. They read all the way until noon. Ezra the priest would read a Bible portion, then students of the Scriptures who were stationed among the people would ask, "Did you understand what he read?" Some folk would say, "No, I never heard that before," or, "I don't know exactly what it means," and they would stop and explain it to them. When faces would light up with understanding, the signal would be given and Ezra would read another segment, and the appointed men would be out there in the crowd to help them understand what he had read.

There began at that time one of the greatest revivals you find recorded in the Bible. Also the order of the scribe began with Ezra, and in time all the scribes began to wear keys. In Christ's day you could see them moving about in the temple area, all wearing keys as the badge of their office.

As the Lord Jesus was instructing His disciples,

He said, "Now that you know who I am, I'm taking the keys away from the scribes, and I'm putting them in your hands, because the key to the Scriptures is your knowing who I am."

My Christian friend, that key is in your hand today. If we withhold the Word, we "bind on earth"; if we give the Word, we "loose on earth." No one man or individual church has the keys to the exclusion of all other believers. We have a responsibility to give out the gospel because it is the only thing that can save people. There is someone around you today, maybe several folk, who are not going to hear the gospel unless *you* give it to them.

The Lord Jesus said, "I am the door. If anyone enters by Me, he will be saved" (John 10:9). It is a wonderful thing to use the keys and open the door for someone who has not heard the gospel before or has not accepted it, and because of your testimony, your use of the keys, he walks in—that is, he comes to faith in Jesus Christ, the Son of the living God!

I close with this little story. It happened in London years ago. One night there was a woman down in the skid row section, the slums of London, dying. She was a prostitute, and she sent her young son to the nearest church to get a rector to come down and talk to her. She said to her boy, "Go get a minister to get me in." So this boy went down to the rectory and knocked on the door. The rector came to the door and said to this little, ragged urchin, "What do you want?"

"My old woman wants you to come and get her in."

"What?"

"My old woman wants you to come and get her in. She's dying."

Then this minister knew what the little fellow meant. He was liberal in his theology and had never preached the gospel. On the way over, he wondered what in the world he would say to her. He couldn't preach what he had been preaching to his congregation—that would get nobody in. Oh, it was scholarly and couched in beautiful language, but it was no good for a dying woman in sin. He thought of what his mother had taught him when he was a boy at her knee. When he reached the house he said to her as she lay there dying, "What is it that you want?"

She said, "I want you to get me in. I'm a sinner. I'm an awful sinner, but I want you to get me in."

He didn't know how to proceed. In a faltering way— he'd never done this before—he turned to John 3:16— that's all he could think of, it's the verse his mother had taught him when he was a boy, so he read it to her, "For God so loved the world that He gave His only begotten Son, that whoever believes in Him should not perish but have everlasting life."

She asked, "Does that mean me?"

"It certainly does, 'whoever' means you and me and anyone."

"Well, I'll believe it. Tell me more."

He knew only John 3:16 for salvation, so he gave it to her again: "'God so loved the world.'"

"Do you suppose He loves me that much?"

"Well, He loves you so much that He gave His Son to die for you."

"Oh," she said, "then I'll trust Him." As she lay dying, a smile came over her face and she said to him, "Minister, thank you for getting me in."

When this preacher was telling about it later, he said, "You know, that night I got two persons in. I got that poor sinful woman in, and I got myself in. I had never been in before."

My friend, that is the use of the keys of the Kingdom of Heaven, and right now the door is open. The Lord Jesus said, "I am the door. If anyone enters by Me, he will be saved" (John 10:9).

Now let me say again, my friend, every believer has the key to the Kingdom of Heaven, and we have the responsibility to use it. If the Spirit of God has made Him real to you, He can also make Him real to the person to whom you are witnessing.

Remember that our Lord said to Peter, "Flesh and blood has not revealed this to you, but My Father who is in heaven." Our part is merely to present His Word—even a single verse like John 3:16 may be enough—and He does the saving.

Oh, what a thrill it is to see someone walk through the open door to come to faith in Jesus Christ, the Son of the living God.

CHAPTER 11

"MAY I WALK WITH YOU?"
(LUKE 24:13–35)

Why is it that the forty-day period between the Resurrection of the Lord Jesus Christ and His Ascension is so often overlooked? Is it because of its brevity? Yet more is recorded in Scripture concerning these forty days than is written of the life of our Lord from His birth to the time He began His ministry when He was thirty years old. Actually these forty days are far more significant to us than those early years before His public ministry. We are robbing ourselves of some of the exceeding riches of His grace by not laying hold of the things revealed to us by Him during this important period.

There are at least two reasons for the importance of the post-Resurrection ministry of Christ. First, these forty days were a continuing witness of His resurrection from the dead. They were a tangible demonstration of it as stated in Acts 1:3: "To whom He also presented Himself alive after His suffering by many infallible proofs, being seen by them during forty days and speaking of the things pertaining to the kingdom of God."

A second reason for the importance of our Lord's post-Resurrection ministry is that we are more vitally related to the life of Christ *after* His resurrection than before. Too many people put a wrong emphasis upon the life of the Lord Jesus as they habitually speak of Him as the Carpenter of Nazareth, the Man of Galilee, and the One who walked the dusty roads. All that is fine, but it is to the living Christ that we are related. "Even though we have known Christ according to the flesh, yet now we know Him thus no longer" (2 Corinthians 5:16).

When Paul wrote in Galatians 2:20, "I have been crucified with Christ; it is no longer I who live, but Christ lives in me," what Christ did he mean? Clearly he was speaking of the resurrected Christ who today is at God's right hand. "Christ lives in me; and the life which I now live in the flesh I live by faith in the Son of God, who loved me and gave Himself for me."

Again we read in 2 Corinthians 5:17, "Therefore, if anyone is in Christ, he is a new creation; old things have passed away; behold, all things have become new." What is meant by that? Simply that believers are no longer related to the first Adam, but to the resurrected Christ. How important that is!

Now behold, two of them were traveling that same day to a village called Emmaus, which was seven miles from Jerusalem. (Luke 24:13)

This road was not as famous as the Jericho road; however, for me it has more meaning. I read that on the Jericho road a man fell among thieves, but on the Emmaus road two humble, unknown disciples met the living Christ face-to-face.

"Unknown?" someone may ask. "One of them was named Cleopas." True, but we do not know who Cleopas was. He and his companion are unknown disciples, and some have suggested that they were man and wife. Whoever they may have been, they were on a little-frequented road, a path just seven miles long. It was not a superhighway, just a narrow, dusty roadway. Yet it was here that Christ made His first public appearance. He had appeared privately to the women in the garden, but He chose a little-known road and two little-known people for His first appearance in a place used by the general public. There followed one of the most remarkable revelations of the living Christ—an interview in which the sublime touched the simple, when the supernatural acted in a natural way.

Two followers of Jesus have left Jerusalem late in the afternoon following the Resurrection, after having heard startling things. They are talking excitedly and frankly, and they are so interested in their conversation that they do not at first notice a stranger who joins them. Finally He interrupts, "What kind of conversation is this that you have with one another as you walk and are sad?" (Luke 24:17).

The word *conversation* here means "discussions." Actually, these two were trying to agree on some reasonable explanation as to why the Lord's body had disappeared. A prophet had been crucified, placed in a conspicuous new tomb, sealed and guarded by Roman soldiers. But now no one could find the body. This news had electrified Jerusalem.

Now notice this fact: Had the enemy been able to produce the body, Christianity would have been sealed forever in that tomb! All that the Lord's adversaries needed were the earthly remains—but they could not find them. Mr. Unbeliever, tell us where the body was!

Along with most of the disciples, these two on the road to Emmaus did not believe that Christ had risen. It is interesting that the followers of Jesus at first were doubters, but before the post-Resurrection ministry of our Lord was ended, these eyewitnesses were thoroughly, joyously convinced that theirs was a risen, living Savior!

Then the one whose name was Cleopas answered and said to Him, "Are You the only stranger in Jerusalem, and have You not known the things which happened there in these days?" (Luke 24:18)

This question raised by Cleopas reveals a sidelight not given by anyone but Dr. Luke. The arrest, crucifixion, and purported resurrection from the dead had stirred Jerusalem. These two people could not believe that there was anyone in the area who did not know about it. It would be like walking down the street in your hometown with a friend and discussing the trip to the moon. A stranger joins you and says, "You mean someone has been to the moon?" You would naturally react. It would be difficult for someone to live in this day and age and not know that someone has been to the moon and back to earth. It was just as incredible to these disciples that someone had not heard about the events of the past few days. Paul in his defense before King Agrippa said that he was persuaded that none of these things were hidden from him "since this thing was not done in a corner" (Acts 26:26). The Crucifixion and Resurrection were not done secretly. They were public news, and everyone in the area was talking about it.

To this, however, the Lord—still unrecognized—simply answered, "What things?"

I think when Christ said this, there was a note of humor in His voice, a twinkle in His eye. Certainly He knew all that was on their hearts, but He was drawing them out.

So they said to Him, "The things concerning Jesus of Nazareth, who was a Prophet mighty in deed and word before God and all the people, and how the chief priests and our rulers delivered Him to be condemned to death, and crucified Him. But we were hoping that it was He who was going to redeem Israel. Indeed, besides all this, today is the third day since these things happened." (Luke 24:19–21)

"Have you not heard about Jesus of Nazareth?" is their incredulous reply. Death had not destroyed the love of these folk for Christ, but it had revealed how limited was their faith. They considered Him simply as "Jesus of Nazareth, who was a Prophet mighty in deed and word before God and all the people."

Note they said Jesus *was* a prophet—they thought He was dead. Then a glimmer of hope lit up their faces: "But we were hoping that it was He who was going to redeem Israel . . . today is the third day since these things happened. Yes, and certain women of our company, who arrived at the tomb early, astonished us" (Luke 24:21, 22).

The other facts soon follow—how the women, "when they did not find His body, they came saying that they had also seen a vision of angels who said He was alive. And certain of those who were with us went to the tomb and found it just as the women had said; but Him they did not see" (Luke 24:23, 24). One can see the depths into which they went. They had loved Him; they had pinned their hopes on Him; but they failed to comprehend the Resurrection. They did not know what had happened, but somehow the body had been taken away. They were not prepared to explain what had taken place, but the fact remained that they thought no one had seen the Lord.

Then He said to them, "O foolish ones, and slow of heart to believe in all that the prophets have spoken!" (Luke 24:25)

This is a very important section, friend. The Lord, in speaking about His Resurrection, did not show them the prints of the nails in His hands to prove it. He referred them to the Scriptures rather than to the nail prints. He told them, "You should have believed what the prophets said." It is well to note the Lord's attitude toward the Bible. The day in which we live is a day of doubt. There are people who are actually saying that you cannot be intelligent and believe the Bible! Many people are afraid that they will not be considered intelligent, so they don't come out flat-footed and say whether they believe the Bible or not. I suppose it is the most subtle and satanic trap of our day to discount the inerrancy and integrity of the Word of God. Christ says a man is a *fool* not to believe it. He gave a unanimous and wholehearted acceptance of the Bible's statements, with no ifs, ands, or buts.

The other day I picked up a seminary professor and took him to a filling station because he had car trouble. As we rode along, I asked him about his school's viewpoint of the inerrancy of Scripture. "Well," he said, "you mean the infallibility of the Bible?" I replied, "Wait a minute, you are arguing semantics. You know what I mean, and I know what you mean. Do you or do you not believe in the inerrancy of Scripture?" Well, he wouldn't make a forthright declaration whether or not he believed it. He wanted to appear intelligent. Frankly, a lot of these men do not have the intestinal fortitude to stand for the Word of God. I think their problem is more intestinal than intellectual!

Now notice that the Lord puts the emphasis upon the Word of God.

"Ought not the Christ to have suffered these things and to enter into His glory?" And beginning at Moses and all the Prophets, He expounded to them in all the Scriptures the things concerning Himself. (Luke 24:26, 27)

He began with the books of Moses and the prophets. Moses and the prophets had spoken of *Him*. His death and resurrection had fulfilled their prophecies. I'd love to have been there that evening, listening to Him, wouldn't you?

Christ says that there are two things essential to the understanding of the Word of God. They are simple but important. First, as verse 25 indicates, we must have faith in the Bible. Christ said, "O foolish ones, and slow of heart to believe in all that the prophets have spoken!" Pascal said, "Human knowledge must be understood to be believed, but divine knowledge must be believed to be understood." I think the Bible is a closed book to the critic and the infidel. He can learn a few facts, but he misses the message. On the other hand, some simple soul whose heart is turned in humble faith to God will be enlightened by the Holy Spirit of God. The eyes of his understanding will be opened.

Some of the great men of the past have come to the pages of Scripture for light and life in the hours of darkness or crisis. It is not smart to ridicule the Bible. The Lord said, "You are a fool not to believe it." I would rather lack sophistication and subtlety than to be a fool.

Then the Lord says that the Bible can only be

divinely understood. Human intellect is simply not enough to comprehend its truths. Verse 45 tells us, "And He opened their understanding, that they might comprehend the Scriptures." Then in 1 Corinthians 2:14 Paul declares, "But the natural man does not receive the things of the Spirit of God, for they are foolishness to him; nor can he know them, because they are spiritually discerned." There are things that are above and beyond human comprehension, and only the Holy Spirit of God can make them real to us. Our prayer ought to be, "Open my eyes, that I may see wondrous things from Your law [Word]" (Psalm 119:18). We should come with a humble attitude to the Word of God. Just because you read the Bible does not mean that you know it. The Holy Spirit of God will have to make it real to you.

> **Then they drew near to the village where they were going, and He indicated that He would have gone farther. But they constrained Him, saying, "Abide with us, for it is toward evening, and the day is far spent." And He went in to stay with them. Now it came to pass, as He sat at the table with them, that He took bread, blessed and broke it, and gave it to them. Then their eyes were opened and they knew Him; and He vanished from their sight.** (Luke 24:28–31)

They wanted Him to stay with them, and He was known to them at the table in the breaking of the bread. Eating around a table is a wonderful time to share the things of Christ. The resurrected, glorified Christ wants to fellowship with those who are His own. And He fellowships only with those who believe in Him.

There is nothing wrong with a church banquet, provided it is not all given over to hearing some soloist or watching a magician or some type of entertainment. We have too many church programs that leave Jesus Christ out. To have true fellowship and blessing, He must be in the midst, breaking bread.

> **And they said to one another, "Did not our heart burn within us while He talked with us on the road, and while He opened the Scriptures to us?" So they rose up that very hour and returned to Jerusalem, and found the eleven and those who were with them gathered together.** (Luke 24:32, 33)

Late as it is, they hurry back over the miles with the wonderful news. And they are greeted by a roomful of overjoyed followers of Jesus, saying, "The Lord is risen indeed, and has appeared to Simon!"

> **And they told about the things that had happened on the road, and how He was known to them in the breaking of bread.** (Luke 24:34, 35)

CHAPTER 12

SECRET OF SERVICE
(JOHN 21)

The scene before us here is a familiar and popular spot, the Sea of Galilee, probably the world's most famous body of water.

It will be of interest to note those present: "Simon Peter, Thomas called the Twin, Nathanael of Cana in Galilee, the sons of Zebedee, and two others of His disciples were together" (John 21:2); an interesting group that might be called the convention of problem children, each a problem in his own way.

First and foremost was Simon Peter—impulsive, impetuous, affectionate, even saying that he would lay down his life for his Lord. Thomas was also present, Thomas the magnificent skeptic, always raising some question or casting some doubt. Then there was Nathanael, a doubter at the beginning of Christ's ministry. Philip came to him and said, "We have found Him of whom Moses in the law, and also the prophets, wrote: Jesus of Nazareth!" Hearing that, Nathanael said, "Can anything good come out of Nazareth?" However, he went with Philip to the Lord Jesus, who said to him, "Before Philip called you, when you were under the fig tree, I saw you." It was then that Nathanael made his first confession:

Nathanael answered and said to Him, "Rabbi, You are the Son of God! You are the King of Israel!" (John 1:49)

Also in the group were James and John, to whom Jesus gave the name "sons of thunder," a name well deserved. There were two other disciples, but their names are not mentioned. And since the Holy Spirit omitted them, let us identify ourselves with them—you and me; we are the two who would probably classify as problem children at the Sea of Galilee.

This group had left Jerusalem and were there in Galilee by commandment, Christ's commandment, relayed by the women who had been at the empty tomb: "Go and tell My brethren to go to Galilee, and there they will see Me" (Matthew 28:10). So here the disciples are at the Sea of Galilee.

I'm Going Fishing

It is springtime, the Passover season. Warm zephyrs from the south make ripples near the shore and whitecaps out on the sea. The surrounding hills are green, and there are wildflowers in profusion. (I once saw it like that a few days after Easter, and I imagine it was even more beautiful two thousand years ago.) They may have waited and waited for the Lord Jesus to come. Peter would be the one to become impatient and, after pacing back and forth and looking up and down the shore, would be the one to say, "I am going fishing." And the six others join him.

They fish all night and catch nothing. This may be the only true fish story that has ever been told! Dr. Scotts calls it the failure of the experts. These men fish all night without catching one fish! They had been restless before, and now they are restless and frustrated. It's easy to fish when you catch fish and frustrating when you don't. They knew how to fish—that's the way they had made their living— but that night of failure was in the will of God for them.

The psalmist says in Psalm 1:3, speaking of God's man, "He shall be like a tree planted by the rivers of water, that brings forth its fruit *in its season.*" The fruitage of man's labor will come forth at a time when it will fit into God's plan and purpose. We are living in a day when everything is measured by the yardstick of materialism. Mathematics is the language of the hour, and to many it is the language of success. When will we learn that spiritual values cannot be determined by figures?

They fished all night and caught nothing! It's hard to fish when the fish are not biting.

The missionary Adoniram Judson had the same experience in Burma when the people were not turning to Christ. His missionary society in New

York wanted to bring him home. They asked, "What are the prospects?" He replied, "The prospects are as bright as the promises of God." Living according to Christ's instructions is the most important thing!

Then on the Sea of Galilee morning dawned, and it must have been a glorious morning. On the morning I was there, I felt like shouting when I thought of this incident.

But when the morning had now come, Jesus stood on the shore; yet the disciples did not know that it was Jesus. (John 21:4)

I think this was a normal experience. He was in His glorified body, and He could be recognized; yet they would have been a distance out on the lake, and in the early morning it would be difficult to identify people on the shore.

Then Jesus said to them, "Children, have you any food?" They answered Him, "No." (John 21:5)

The Greek word for "children" is almost like saying, "Sirs." It is not a term of endearment like "little children" in 1 John. Their answer is a short "No." It's amazing how emphatic one can be and how little one likes to talk about failure. Although they answer Him, they don't want to talk about it. If they had a good catch of fish, they all would be showing Him how long they were.

This is a question He is bound to ask every one of us someday: "Did you catch anything? What did you do for people down there on earth?" I hope your answer will not be the same as theirs, "No, I didn't catch a thing."

And He said to them, "Cast the net on the right side of the boat, and you will find some." So they cast, and now they were not able to draw it in because of the multitude of fish. (John 21:6)

The whole thought here is that He directs the lives of His own. He gives the instructions, and they are to be obeyed. When they fish according to His instruction, the net fills. Notice, the net does not break even though it is full.

There was another time recorded by Luke when Peter caught a miraculous number of fish. It was in the early days of Jesus' ministry, and He was calling Peter to be a fisher of men. That time the net broke. I think Peter was to realize that many would follow Jesus, but they would not all be believers—the net would break and many fish would swim away. This time the net did not break but was drawn to land, "full of large fish." Peter is going to be called to feed the sheep and feed the lambs. With what? With the Word of God. With the gospel of a risen, glorified Christ. The gospel will not only save, but it will hold. Even in their failures, believers are kept by the power of God through faith.

It's the Lord!

We see in this incident that Jesus Christ has a purpose for His own. He wants to direct our lives. If we obey, He will bless and have wonderful fellowship with us. He is the Lord of our wills.

> **Therefore that disciple whom Jesus loved said to Peter, "It is the Lord!" Now when Simon Peter heard that it was the Lord, he put on his outer garment (for he had removed it), and plunged into the sea.** (John 21:7)

John has a spiritual perception that Simon Peter doesn't have. Three years before, Jesus had called them to follow Him, and perhaps it was at this same spot. But now they have gone back to fishing, and the Lord calls them again to fish for the souls of men.

Peter may not have the discernment of John, but have you noticed that at every opportunity he gets close to the Lord? The other men sit in the boat and wait until they get to shore. Not Simon Peter. He can't wait! He wants to be close to his Lord. I love this man.

> **But the other disciples came in the little boat (for they were not far from land, but about two hundred cubits), dragging the net with fish. Then, as soon as they had come to land, they saw a fire of coals there, and fish laid on it, and bread.** (John 21:8, 9)

What a welcome sight for tired, hungry men! Oh, how our Lord loves His own!

Jesus said to them, "Bring some of the fish which you have just caught." Simon Peter went up and dragged the net to land, full of large fish, one hundred and fifty-three; and although there were so many, the net was not broken. (John 21:10, 11)

Notice that although Jesus had fish laid on a bed of coals for their breakfast on the shore of Galilee, He also asks for some of the fish they had caught. He accepts their service. When they have fished at His command, He accepts what they bring. What blessed fellowship there is in this kind of service!

There by the Sea of Galilee the fire was made; the coals had burned their course. When the men arrived on shore, cold, wet and hungry, Jesus said, "Come and dine," or, "Come and eat breakfast." What an invitation! The resurrected Christ had prepared their meal.

Jesus did command, "Go into all the world and preach the gospel" (Mark 16:15), but He would rather you come and have breakfast with Him before you go. The lovely part is that the resurrected Lord, God Himself, feeds them. If only we would sit today and let Him feed us! He wants to feed His own.

Now here on the shore of Galilee He has prepared breakfast for them, and they sit down to a hearty meal. You will recall that the last time this group had eaten together was in the Upper Room—and what a contrast that meal was with this! The other was before His crucifixion; this is after His death and resurrection. On the former occasion they were in an upstairs room; now they are out of doors. Before they were in the city; now they are away from the city's crowds. Before they were conversing excitedly; now there is great quietness. In the Upper Room the shadow of the Cross was upon them, and in the flush of the moment they were asking many questions. Peter said, "Where are You going? Let me go with You—I will lay down my life for You!" Thomas said, "We do not know where You are going, and how can we know the way?" Philip said, "Show us the Father, and it is sufficient for us." And Judas, not Iscariot, said, "Lord, how is it that You will manifest Yourself to us and not to the world?"

How different is this meal on the seashore, which was eaten in silence—not even the Lord Jesus said anything. When He had told them, "Come and eat breakfast," not one of them asked, "Who are You?" knowing that it was the Lord. The resurrected and glorified Jesus was the same Jesus, though there was a difference born of the Resurrection, and they would not be so familiar with Him now.

And so these men are eating breakfast with Him. They know that He is the risen and glorified Christ, and they say nothing. This is a men's meeting. I call attention to this fact, for we are living in a day when Christianity is looked upon as a woman's interest. But in its beginnings we find this group of virile fishermen, rugged in life and rugged in faith.

> **So when they had eaten breakfast, Jesus said to Simon Peter, "Simon, son of Jonah, do you love Me more than these?" He said to Him, "Yes, Lord; You know that I love You." He said to him, "Feed My lambs."** (John 21:15)

Here is something very important. After the meal, the Lord Jesus questioned Peter three times. Peter answered three times, and on the basis of that the Lord Jesus commissioned him three times.

Why three times? Why not just once? We are not sure that we know, but three times Peter had denied Christ publicly, and three times he makes an affirmation. This, then, is the restoration of Simon Peter to service.

There are those who contend that this elevates Peter above the other apostles. There is not a word to prove that. Because of his denial, Peter had fallen and was in disgrace, and in this act the Lord brought him back to the level of service with the others. He is brought back publicly to the position which he had occupied before.

The Lord Jesus had appeared to him privately (1 Corinthians 15:8). Details of that are not recorded, but it was then that he was restored to fellowship by his repentance. But on this occasion the Lord restores him to service.

Peter Is Questioned

Now look briefly at the mechanics of this passage. There are three interrogations by the Lord. There are three declarations of Simon Peter. There are three exhortations or imperatives of the Lord Jesus. While the three interrogations are similar, each of them is different. As to the declarations of Peter, the first two are identical, but the third statement adds, "Lord, You know all things; You know that I love You." The three exhortations of the Lord are all different. First, He tells Simon Peter, "Be grazing My lambs." Second, "Shepherd My sheep," and third, "Be grazing My sheep." You will want to consider the three aspects of this questioning.

Jesus must have looked across the dying embers of that fire upon which He had prepared their breakfast and straight into the eyes of Simon Peter as He said, "Simon, son of Jonah, do you love Me more than these?"

Note the significance of his name. To begin with He called him Simon. That is interesting—Simon son of Jonah—why did He call him Simon? You may recall that when the Lord Jesus first met this man, his brother Andrew had brought him to Jesus, and when Jesus looked at him, He said in effect, "You are Simon the son of Jonah. You shall be called Cephas." Cephas is the Aramaic word for "Rock Man." In Greek it is *Petros*, and that name clung to him. We find that over in Caesarea Philippi, when he gave that marvelous testimony concerning the Lord Jesus Christ and said, "You are the Christ, the

Son of the living God," the Lord Jesus said in effect, "Blessed are you, Simon [He goes back to his old name] . . . you will be called Peter because you are going to be a Rock Man from here on. You will be a man who will stand for something, but right now there is still a question." And so the Lord reminds him of his old name.

If you and I today think that we are somebody important, perhaps He would like to tell us just who we really are! Perhaps we are like Simon, the wishy-washy, mollycoddle fellow who tried to please everybody, who attempted to boast and was filled with pride. Our Lord dealt with him and settled him quietly when He said, "Simon [his old name], do you love Me more than these?"

Words for Love

There are three words in the Greek language that are translated into the English by the one word *love*. Perhaps, my friend, you are not aware of the fact that the English language is a beggar for words. We have the one word *love*, and that is about all. Hollywood today would give a million dollars for another word. The best they have done is *sex*, and that is pretty low. But Greek is a language that is versatile; it is flexible. They have several words for this thing called love.

The first word we will look at is the word *eros*. In the use of this word the Greeks degraded the meaning of love by personifying it. The fact of the matter is they made "Eros" a god and put together in combination the names Aphrodite and Eros. Today we know these names better as Venus and Cupid. The latter are the Roman names, but they are the same, as the Greeks are the ones who started this idea with Aphrodite and Eros. *Eros* is a word of sensuality, and we do believe that the Hollywood word *sex*, which has really been put into high gear today, would best express what the Greeks had in mind. But this word *eros* is never used in the Word of God.

There is another Greek word, *phileo*, and it means "friendship." It has to do with the affection and the emotion in a human relationship at its very best usage. We get our word *philanthropic* from it, and *Philadelphia* comes from it—Philadelphia, the "city of brotherly love." And that is a word that is used in Scripture.

The third Greek word for love is *agapao*—it is a word of dignity, the highest and noblest word and, in connection with this verse, there is always the note of worth; that either the lover or the beloved is "worthy" of love. I am sure this is a Bible word, for we see it used in John 3:16: "For God so *loved* the world that He gave His only begotten Son." Again, Paul said, "Who *loved* me, and gave Himself for me." John said, "We *love* Him, because He first *loved* us." These are instances where this word appears, and it is the word Christ used twice with Simon Peter.

Now notice that our Lord's first question to Peter is, "Do you love Me more than these men love Me?" You will recall that the Lord Jesus said, the last time they were in the Upper Room, "One of you will betray Me" (John 13:21). Peter doubtless thought, *Yes, I haven't trusted this crowd either*. But to the Lord he said, "There is one fellow here on whom You can depend—You can count on me." Obviously Peter didn't know himself. But now the Lord Jesus says to Peter, "Simon, son of Jonah, do you love Me with divine love more than these other disciples love Me with divine love?" That is essentially what He is saying. Now listen to Simon Peter. "Yes, Lord; You know that I love You." Here Simon will not use the word *agapao* but comes down to the word *phileo*. In other words, "You know that I have an affection for You."

There are many who find fault with Peter for this, but he did the best he could. You see, the love of God, the *agapao* love, is shed abroad in our hearts by the Holy Spirit who is given to us, and Peter was not yet filled with the Holy Spirit. Christ had not yet ascended and the Holy Spirit had not yet indwelt believers, so this big, rugged fisherman expressed the deepest affection that was in his heart for the Lord Jesus Christ.

But also, if you want my opinion, this man is through boasting. Never again will he brag of what he will do. Never again will you hear him saying, "I am going to do something big for the Lord." From here on he is going to do something big, but he is not going to say anything about it. He comes to the low plane, "I have an affection for You."

Our Lord did not censure Simon Peter for failure to rise to the heights of love. No, He recommissioned him and gave him his first imperative, saying, "Feed

My lambs," or better still, "Be grazing My baby
lambs (My tiny lambs)." These are the new Christians who, regardless of age, are baby lambs to Him.
And if you love the Lord Jesus Christ, you will want
to feed His lambs. Each Lord's day there are millions of Sunday school teachers who feed a host of
His little lambs, and they do it because they love
Him.

Now we come to the second interrogation. The
Lord Jesus asks a second time, "Simon, son of
Jonah, do you love Me?" No longer does our Lord
make the comparison with the other disciples; He
makes it purely personal: "Can you, Simon, say
from your heart that you love Me with a divine
love?"

Again Simon Peter cannot ascend the heights. He
answers as on the first occasion, "Lord, You know
that I have a human affection for You," and this
comes from his heart, doubtless every fiber of his
being trembling at the words. The Lord does not
criticize him but adds a second commission, "Tend"
or "Shepherd My sheep." That means to discipline
by giving direction.

Today we have it all mixed up; we try to discipline
the young Christians and feed the old ones. The
Lord said, "Feed the young ones and discipline the
old ones."

An anxious father asked, "How can I bring up my
boy in the way he should go?" and the answer was
given him, "By going in that way yourself."

Another has expressed it poetically:

'Twas a sheep, not a lamb, that strayed away,
  In the parable Jesus told;
A grown-up sheep, that had gone astray,
  From the ninety and nine in the fold.

Out on the hillside, out in the cold,
  'Twas a sheep the Good Shepherd sought;
And back to the flock, safe into the fold,
  'Twas a sheep the Good Shepherd brought.

Why for the sheep should we earnestly long,
  And as earnestly hope and pray?
Because there is danger, if they go wrong,
  They will lead the lambs astray.
For the lambs will follow the sheep, you know,
  Wherever the sheep may stray;
When the sheep go wrong, it will not be long
  Till the lambs are as wrong as they.

And so with the sheep we earnestly plead,
  For the sake of the lambs today;
If the sheep are lost, what terrible cost
  Some lambs will have to pay.

—Author unknown

It is not Junior, but his father, who needs the discipline.

The third interrogation reveals an interesting dealing of the Lord with Simon Peter. Our Lord dropped down and used the same word that Simon had been obliged to use and said, "Simon, son of Jonah, do you have a human affection for Me?" It grieved Peter because the Lord asked him this for the third time, and with a burst of emotion he said in effect, "You know that I love You. I wish with all my heart I could say that I have a divine love for You, and I think I do. But I have found out that I cannot trust myself anymore, for I make such big statements but do so little. Lord, I am sorry that it is necessary for You to come down to my plane of *phileo* love, but it is the best I can do. You know my heart. You know all things. You know I love You." Then the Lord Jesus gives him the third imperative: "Be grazing My sheep."

There is much church activity today, but why is there so little Bible study in the pulpit? Do not misunderstand me when I say this, but my conviction is that there is little study of the Word of God because we must first answer Christ's question, "Do you love Me?" Until that is answered in the affirmative, the commission "Feed My sheep" will not be given to us.

We must remember that the Lord Jesus commissioned Simon Peter on one basis alone—"Do you love Me?" This is the badge of Christianity. The Roman officials sent men to spy out the Christians, and Tertullian writes that when the spies returned, their report was that the Christians were strange folk; they had no idols, but they spoke of One who was absent by the name of Jesus, and how they loved Him! And how they loved one another! That is the report made of the Christians of that day. I wonder how a report made of the people in your church and my church would compare.

Listen to Paul writing to the Corinthians: "If any

man love not the Lord Jesus, let him be anathema. I can have all knowledge, but if I have not love, I am nothing" (1 Corinthians 16:22 and 13:2 KJV). You and I are under this acid test: Do we love Him?

The greatest drives in the world are not intellectual. Rather, they are drives of the heart. Christianity is a matter of the heart. And we must start right —"with the heart one believes unto righteousness." The church today needs a baptism of emotion; it needs real and genuine tears coming from the heart that can say, "Lord Jesus, You know that I love You." Christianity is a love affair. Peter wrote, "Whom having not seen, you love."

In Portsmouth, Virginia, back in antebellum days, there was a famous blind preacher by the name of Waddell. Since this was a seacoast town, late one Sunday afternoon a sailing vessel put into port, and the sailors went ashore. The captain and three of the sailors were Christians and seemingly by accident went into the church where Waddell was preaching.

That night his text was the same as the one used here, and he concluded with this question, "Can each one of you who is a member say at this time, 'Lord Jesus, You know that I love You'?" A hush went over the congregation. Then one of the sailors, forgetting where he was, broke the silence and cried out with all of the enthusiasm of his young heart, "Lord Jesus, You know everything. You know that I love You!"

In my own experience I vividly recall a night in Georgia, walking together with a fellow seminary student and talking enthusiastically about what we were learning concerning our Lord Jesus Christ. Suddenly we stopped in our tracks. We had reached the top of the hill, and before us was the rising moon—oh, that Georgia moon, how beautiful it was! We just stood there and watched silently. Finally my friend said, "*He* made that!"

Then he said something else that has been very helpful to me. He told me that every night before going to sleep, he told the Lord Jesus, "I *love* You."

My friend, loving Him is a wonderful experience. It is, as Peter wrote in his first epistle, "joy inexpressible and full of glory!" And it is the secret of having a ministry that God can and will use.

CHAPTER 13

WHERE IS CHRIST NOW AND WHAT IS HE DOING?

W e in Bible-teaching churches have remembered Christ's virgin birth. In fact, we have spoken eloquently of it. We talk about His spotless life; we give attention to His miraculous earthly ministry; we will even talk of His substitutionary death and of His bodily resurrection. We marvel at the wonderful compassionate Man our Lord revealed Himself to be when He walked among us in the days of His flesh. But from there on it gets hazy. From there on it seems that we are unsure what He is doing now and even not quite certain where He is. But the Scripture is crystal clear on Christ's present position, and the Word of God is lucid concerning His present occupation.

Present Position of Christ

First of all, note the present position of Christ. Now there isn't any use going to Bethlehem during the Christmas season—friends, He is not there.

Where is He? He is in the glory at the right hand of God the Father. Will you notice how the Word of God presents this to us? When Dr. Luke concluded the third Gospel, this is what he wrote:

Now it came to pass, while He blessed them, that He was parted from them and carried up into heaven. (Luke 24:51)

Let me remind you that the Gospel of Luke was written by a medical doctor of the first century who used more medical terms than Hippocrates, the founder of medicine. Dr. Luke says that Christ was received into heaven, but he doesn't leave it there. He began the Book of Acts, which he also wrote, by saying:

The former account I made, O Theophilus, of all that Jesus began both to do and teach, until the day in which He was taken up, after He through the Holy Spirit had given commandments to the apostles whom He had chosen. (Acts 1:1, 2)

In other words, "I gave you a former account or treatise in which I told you what Jesus began to do and to teach. Now I'm going to continue where I left off and tell you what He is doing right now." And when you enter the Book of Acts, you find out that Simon Peter on the Day of Pentecost and on other occasions bore testimony of what Christ is presently doing. Paul and the other apostles said in substance, "These things happening down here are because

Jesus is busy up yonder." Oh, how important that is!

And when you come to the Book of the Revelation, written by John, he says:

And when I saw Him, I fell at His feet as dead. But He laid His right hand on me, saying to me, "Do not be afraid; I am the First and the Last." (Revelation 1:17)

It was approaching A.D. 100 when John wrote the last books of the Bible, and though Jesus had died about seventy years earlier, John saw Him alive and had contact with the living Christ. My beloved, that's the testimony of the Word of God. The One born about two thousand years ago, who died on a cross, was buried and rose again bodily, is alive today. Oh, how eloquent Scripture is on this. Look with me at the Book of Hebrews:

But this Man, after He had offered one sacrifice for sins forever, sat down at the right hand of God, from that time waiting till His enemies are made His footstool. (Hebrews 10:12, 13)

Therefore we also, since we are surrounded by so great a cloud of witnesses, let us lay aside every weight, and the sin which so easily ensnares us, and let us run with endurance the race that is set before us, looking unto Jesus, the author and finisher of our faith, who for the joy that was set before Him en-

dured the cross, despising the shame, and has sat down at the right hand of the throne of God. (Hebrews 12:1, 2)

Stephen, the first martyr, when he was being stoned, said:

"Look! I see the heavens opened and the Son of Man standing at the right hand of God!" (Acts 7:56)

Saul, that brilliant young Pharisee (later called Paul), who did not believe in Christ's resurrection, who hated Jesus with a vengeance, met Him on the Damascus Road and made the discovery of his life. When he said, "Who are You, Lord?" Jesus answered, "I am Jesus, whom You are persecuting." Paul found out that He was indeed alive and still busy. Paul wrote later to the believers at Rome:

Who is he who condemns? It is Christ who died, and furthermore is also risen, who is even at the right hand of God, who also makes intercession for us. (Romans 8:34)

Paul says He is at God's right hand.

I think Annie Johnson Flint has expressed it in a wonderful way in her poem, *The Way of the Cross*:

Some of us stay at the cross.
Some of us wait at the tomb.
Quickened and raised with Christ,
Yet lingering still in the gloom.

Some of us bide at the Passover Feast
With Pentecost all unknown,
The triumphs of grace in the heavenly place
That our Lord has made our own.

If the Christ who died had stopped at the cross,
His work had been incomplete.
If the Christ who was buried had stayed in the tomb,
He had only known defeat.

But the way of the cross never stops at the cross,
And the way of the tomb leads on
To victorious grace in the heavenly place
Where the risen Lord has gone.

This moment at this split second, Jesus is at God's right hand. What is He doing?

Present Occupation of Christ

His work is so varied today. If you get the impression, when the Bible says He is seated at God's right hand, that He's twiddling His thumbs, I'm afraid you've missed the entire point. The fact that He is seated at God's right hand means He occupies the place of honor. And in reference to His work on earth, it means that it is complete. He sat down.

In my office you would see my desk covered with work to be done. I've never been able to sit down and say, "It's finished." I have a notion that you experience this in your life also. We never reach a day when we can say, "It's finished." But when the Lord Jesus died on the cross, it was finished. All the work had been done for your salvation and mine. He sat down at God's right hand. But if you think that means He is doing nothing, you are wrong. I do not have time to mention all the varied ministries of our Lord today, but I do want to mention three that are very important.

Intercessor—He Is Interceding for Us

First of all, He is an intercessor for those who are His own. He prays for those of us who belong to Him. You have the picture given in John 17, which I call the Lord's prayer. There we hear Him praying to the Father about the believers, the body of believers He calls His church. Consider this prayer for just a moment.

> "I pray for them. I do not pray for the world but for those whom You have given Me, for they are Yours. . . . Sanctify them by Your truth. Your word is truth. As You sent Me into the world, I also have sent them into the world. And for their sakes I sanctify Myself, that they also may be sanctified by the truth. I do not pray for these alone, but also for those who will believe in Me through their word." (John 17:9, 17–20)

Notice that He wasn't praying only for the apostles but also for those who would believe on Him through their witness. One of the things that He does today is to pray for those who are His own. He prays for *you*! Remember that He said to Simon Peter:

> **"Simon, Simon! Indeed, Satan has asked for you, that he may sift you as wheat. But I have prayed for you, that your faith should not fail; and when you have returned to Me, strengthen your brethren."** (Luke 22:31, 32)

Jesus told Peter he was going to have a rough time. In other words, "You are going to fail, Simon Peter, but I have prayed that your faith will not fail"—and it did not fail, because Jesus prayed. And, my friend, that's the reason I have made it through up to this point—because He has been up there praying for me. And that's the reason you have made it through to this moment. He's up there praying for you.

Let's think about Romans 8:34 again. "Who is he who condemns?" Who condemns any sinner who has trusted Jesus? "It is Christ who died, and furthermore is also risen, who is even at the right hand of God, who also makes intercession for us." Do you know the reason today that a believer is safe down here? It's not because he's a solid, strong believer. It is because he has a mighty Intercessor up yonder praying for him. Our Lord Jesus prays for those who are His own.

> **Therefore He is also able to save to the uttermost those who come to God through Him, since He always lives to make intercession for them.** (Hebrews 7:25)

Beloved, if He saves you He can hold on to you. He's able to save to the uttermost because He's making intercession for you.

Advocate—He Pleads Our Case

He has a second ministry. He is performing it right now. He is our *Advocate*.

My little children, these things I write to you, so that you may not sin. And if anyone sins, we have an Advocate with the Father, Jesus Christ the righteous. And He Himself is the propitiation for our sins, and not for ours only but also for the whole world. (1 John 2:1, 2)

When a Christian sins, Christ immediately goes to court for him. And the reason He must go to court is because there is the accuser of the brethren present. Satan is right there probably to say, among other things, "You don't mean to tell me that You have saved that person down there, that failing Christian?" The Lord Jesus Christ would say, "Yes, he's failing, and I'm ashamed of him. But here are the wounds in My hands. I died for Him." Oh, friend, He's our Advocate to plead our case up yonder! Our sins are very well known up there.

You have set our iniquities before You, our secret sins in the light of Your countenance. (Psalm 90:8)

Dr. Lewis Sperry Chafer used to say, "What is secret sin down here is open scandal in heaven." If you are a Christian and think, *I've done something and nobody knows anything about it,* they're talking about it all over heaven today. Everybody up there knows, and you ought to be thankful that you have an Advocate there to stand up for you. He is there to go to court for us today.

For Christ has not entered the holy places made with hands, which are copies of the true, but into heaven itself, now to appear in the presence of God for us. (Hebrews 9:24)

He is our Advocate. And when we sin, the thing that we are asked to do is this:

If we confess our sins, He is faithful and just to forgive us our sins and to cleanse us from all unrighteousness. (1 John 1:9)

He forgives us. But He has had to go before the Father and plead for us. So we are to confess and forsake our sins.

Judge—He Examines Our Works

Now I come to the third and last point in this message about what our Lord Jesus is doing right now. He is the Judge of His own. That's the great truth of the Book of the Revelation. I have come to the conclusion in a further study of this book that

Christ is the great center of it, but also that He is a Judge from the beginning of Revelation to the end of the book. He is presented in the Gospels as a Savior, but in the Book of the Revelation He's presented as a Judge. That's the picture. And that's entirely omitted and neglected by the contemporary church. He judges the church. He judges believers. Oh, He doesn't haul them into court. This is a family affair. They are His own, and He does the judging; He holds them accountable for what they do.

We always speak of the first vision presented to us in the Revelation as being a vision of the glorified Christ. That is true, but that's not the whole story by any means. Not only is He glorified, He is presented as a priest.

Then I turned to see the voice that spoke with me. And having turned I saw seven golden lampstands, and in the midst of the seven lampstands One like the Son of Man, clothed with a garment down to the feet and girded about the chest with a golden band. (Revelation 1:12, 13)

That's the picture of Him as High Priest, ministering before God.

Then will you notice something else that's here? Back in the Book of Leviticus the high priest was a judge. You'll find that Israel was a theocracy, and every case was to be brought to the priests and to the high priest of that day. He was the Supreme Court. Our Lord Jesus is today the Great High Priest of the church. He not only is our Intercessor and our Advocate—He has not only made a new way for us, He not only gives us access—but today as the Great High Priest He also judges His church.

His head and hair were white like wool, as white as snow, and His eyes like a flame of fire. (Revelation 1:14)

That's judgment. He's looking at those who are His own, because every man's work will be tested by fire.

His feet were like fine brass, as if refined in a furnace, and His voice as the sound of many waters. (Revelation 1:15)

Brass also speaks of judgment. It is the material from which the Old Testament brazen altar was made, where the sin question was settled.

He had in His right hand seven stars, out of His mouth went a sharp two-edged sword. (Revelation 1:16)

The sword represents His Word: "For the word of God is living and powerful, and sharper than any two-edged sword." (Hebrews 4:12). He judges by His Word—He does so today. How do you measure up to His Word? The lampstands among which we see Him standing as the Great High Priest represent the church. And that's where He is today.

John's reaction was tremendous.

His countenance was like the sun shining in its strength. And when I saw Him, I fell at His feet as dead. But He laid His right hand on me, saying to me, "Do not be afraid; I am the First and the Last." (Revelation 1:16, 17)

John said that when he saw Him, he fell at His feet as dead. Yet this is the man who yonder in the Upper Room had reclined on His bosom! He was so familiar with Him that he could rebuke Him, but when he saw Him as the glorified Christ, he fell down before Him as dead.

There are a great many people today who talk like this, "Oh, when I get into His presence, it's going to be wonderful! I'm just going to go up to Him and I'm going to thank Him and talk things over with Him." My friend, you and I will probably spend the first million years down on our faces before Him. That's how exalted He is today.

You see, the high priest of the Old Testament faithfully went into the tabernacle and stood before that golden altar which speaks of prayer; but not only did he make intercession, that high priest also came to the golden lampstand—which is the most glorious picture of Christ in the Old Testament— and he took scissors and trimmed the wick when it smoked. And when one of the lights wouldn't burn right, he used snuffers to extinguish it and then put another light in its place.

The golden lampstands speak of Christ's present work in heaven in maintaining the lights. That's where the Lord Jesus is today, standing in the midst of the lampstands, the Church, representing those of us who are His own. We are to be the light of the world, and He begins to trim the wick that the light might be brighter. He reaches in and turns and fills the lamps with oil, speaking of the filling of the Holy Spirit. He's busy today, my beloved.

The lampstand in the tabernacle is a picture of Him. The Lord Jesus said, "I am the light of the world." But He also said, "You are the light of the world." He is gone now—He has passed out of sight and into the presence of the Father, and we know Him no longer after the flesh. We know Him no longer as the little Baby born in Bethlehem nor as the Man hanging on a cross. He today is the glorified Christ, the Light of the world. But He says to us, "You are lights in the world."

I do not mean to be irreverent, but He's in the power and light business today. He is giving power, the filling of the Spirit, to His own. He is making His believers down here lights in the world. This is so important that it's repeated again and again and again in the New Testament. When Paul was converted, the Lord Jesus said he would be a light to the Gentiles. Oh, what a light he has been to us! Notice what Paul wrote to the various churches.

For you were once darkness, but now you are light in the Lord. Walk as children of light. (Ephesians 5:8)

You are all sons of light and sons of the day. We are not of the night nor of darkness. (1 Thessalonians 5:5)

That you may become blameless and harmless, children of God without fault in the midst of a crooked and perverse generation, among whom you shine as lights in the world. (Philippians 2:15)

When you and I go out at night, looking up we can see the stars in a black sky. When He looks down from heaven, He sees the inky blackness of this world, and He sees those of us who are His own as lights. He is in the midst of us—trimming, filling, adjusting, bringing us into another position where we can give better light. That's what He is doing today.

His own must be usable. We must be expendable. We must be bent to His will. We must be pliable. We must be yielded to Him. We must be willing to be lights in the world.

His work is both negative and positive. It's negative—He punishes sins. Paul, talking about the Lord's table says,

But let a man examine himself, and so let him eat of the bread and drink of the cup. For he who eats and drinks in an unworthy manner eats and drinks judgment to himself, not discerning the Lord's body. For this reason many are weak and sick among you, and many sleep. For if we would judge ourselves, we would not be judged. But when we are judged, we are chastened by the Lord, that we may not be condemned with the world. (1 Corinthians 11:28–32)

One of the things the Lord Jesus does is to move in among believers today inspecting the lights, and as He finds a lamp that's burning so very dimly, is giving off smoke and is not a blessing at all, He begins to trim. If that individual will judge himself, the Lord Jesus won't judge him. But if that individual won't judge himself, then He will judge.

My friend, do you want to know if you are a child of God or not? Here's a sure test. If you can get by with sin, you are not His child. Our Lord is in the midst of the lampstands, and when one of His lights won't burn, He trims it, always trims it. He won't let you get by with sin if you are His. He'll take you to the woodshed. He hasn't read the new books on discipline!

And when the child of God sins, the thing to do is confess it to Him. And if he will not confess and be corrected, then this Great High Priest picks up His snuffer, and He puts the light out—that is, He removes him:

"Remember therefore from where you have fallen; repent and do the first works, or else I will come to you quickly and remove your lampstand from its place—unless you repent." (Revelation 2:5)

That's the negative side.

There's a positive side. Consider this for just a moment.

Do you not know that those who run in a race all run, but one receives the prize? Run in

such a way that you may obtain it. And everyone who competes for the prize is temperate in all things. Now they do it to obtain a perishable crown, but we for an imperishable crown. Therefore I run thus: not with uncertainty. Thus I fight: not as one who beats the air. But I discipline my body and bring it into subjection, lest, when I have preached to others, I myself should become disqualified. (1 Corinthians 9:24–27)

Now Paul the apostle doesn't mean he will lose his salvation. He means that after he has preached to others, he doesn't want to hear the Lord say to him, "You have failed me, Paul. You were not light in the world. I made you to be light."

So the Christian life to Paul was serious business. It was like training for a race. And Paul says, "I even discipline my body, and I do it in order that I might obtain a crown. I want to be approved of Him."

The Christian life, friends, is not a sideline. It's not a hobby. It's not something to occupy your spare time. It's not a game that you play. Somebody has said that in our day athletics are played as if they were a business, but the Christian life is lived as if it were a game and not reality. But that's not the way Paul lived the Christian life. He was out training. He wanted to win, and he intended to win. He did not intend to lose.

But there are a lot of Christians doing just the opposite. They're not winning because it's merely a little game with them. The church has become, to some people, only a religious club, and that applies to both liberals and conservatives. Church is where they go once a week if it's convenient and makes them feel good.

My beloved, the Christian life is a gymnasium where there's rigorous training and where you develop spiritual muscles. I hear a great deal today about how we ought to train leaders. But the purpose of any Christian training should not be primarily to develop leadership but to develop lights in this world.

Our Lord wants us to be lights. The Lord made Paul a light and was able to use him in an extraordinary way. On one occasion He caught him up to heaven and gave him revelations that he could not speak about. Paul wrote:

And lest I should be exalted above measure by the abundance of the revelations, a thorn in the flesh was given to me, a messenger of Satan to buffet me, lest I be exalted above measure. (2 Corinthians 12:7)

The Lord gave Paul that to keep him humble. It seems that God put a reflector on Paul so he would be a bright light. And God will send you and me troubles in order that we might be better lights in the world.

This very moment, my friend, Christ is busy at the right hand of God, at the place of honor. Although He has finished His work for our redemption, as our Great High Priest He still ministers to us who are His own. Walking in the midst of the lampstands, He is our Intercessor, our Advocate, and our Judge. Oh, my friend,

Let us lay aside every weight, and the sin which so easily ensnares us, and let us run with endurance the race that is set before us, looking unto Jesus, the author and finisher of our faith, who for the joy that was set before Him endured the cross, despising the shame, and has sat down at the right hand of the throne of God. (Hebrews 12:1, 2)